COMPACT *Research*

Gambling Addiction

Addictions

ReferencePoint
Press®

San Diego, CA

Other books in the Compact Research Addictions set:

Heroin Addiction
Internet and Social Media Addiction
Sex and Pornography Addictions
Synthetic Drug Addiction

*For a complete list of titles please visit www.referencepointpress.com.

Gambling Addiction

Christine Wilcox

Addictions

ReferencePoint Press®

San Diego, CA

© 2015 ReferencePoint Press, Inc.
Printed in the United States

For more information, contact:
ReferencePoint Press, Inc.
PO Box 27779
San Diego, CA 92198
www.ReferencePointPress.com

Picture credits:
Maury Aaseng: 32–34, 46–48, 60–61, 74–75
Thinkstock Images: 13, 17

LIBRARY OF CONGRESS CATALOGING-IN-PUBLICATION DATA

Wilcox, Christine.
    Gambling Addiction/by Christine Wilcox
        pages cm.--(Compact research series)
Includes bibliographical references and index.
ISBN-13: 978-1-60152-758-5 (hardback)
ISBN-10: 1-60152-758-6 (hardback)
    1. Gambling Addiction--Juvenile literature. 2. Addiction

2014037119

Contents

Foreword

As modern civilization continues to evolve, its ability to create, store, distribute, and access information expands exponentially. The explosion of information from all media continues to increase at a phenomenal rate. By 2020 some experts predict the worldwide information base will double every seventy-three days. While access to diverse sources of information and perspectives is paramount to any democratic society, information alone cannot help people gain knowledge and understanding. Information must be organized and presented clearly and succinctly in order to be understood. The challenge in the digital age becomes not the creation of information, but how best to sort, organize, enhance, and present information.

ReferencePoint Press developed the *Compact Research* series with this challenge of the information age in mind. More than any other subject area today, researching current issues can yield vast, diverse, and unqualified information that can be intimidating and overwhelming for even the most advanced and motivated researcher. The *Compact Research* series offers a compact, relevant, intelligent, and conveniently organized collection of information covering a variety of current topics ranging from illegal immigration and deforestation to diseases such as anorexia and meningitis.

The series focuses on three types of information: objective single-author narratives, opinion-based primary source quotations, and facts and statistics. The clearly written objective narratives provide context and reliable background information. Primary source quotes are carefully selected and cited, exposing the reader to differing points of view, and facts and statistics sections aid the reader in evaluating perspectives. Presenting these key types of information creates a richer, more balanced learning experience.

For better understanding and convenience, the series enhances information by organizing it into narrower topics and adding design features that make it easy for a reader to identify desired content. For example, in *Compact Research: Illegal Immigration*, a chapter covering the economic impact of illegal immigration has an objective narrative explaining the various ways the economy is impacted, a balanced section of numerous primary source quotes on the topic, followed by facts and full-color illustrations to encourage evaluation of contrasting perspectives.

The ancient Roman philosopher Lucius Annaeus Seneca wrote, "It is quality rather than quantity that matters." More than just a collection of content, the *Compact Research* series is simply committed to creating, finding, organizing, and presenting the most relevant and appropriate amount of information on a current topic in a user-friendly style that invites, intrigues, and fosters understanding.

Gambling Addiction at a Glance

Gambling Addiction Defined

Gambling addiction is an uncontrollable urge to gamble despite negative consequences.

Causes of Gambling Addiction

Gambling addiction is caused by genetic vulnerability, environmental influences, and frequent exposure to gambling.

False Beliefs

Gambling addicts frequently have false beliefs and superstitions that contribute to their addiction, such as a belief that if they gamble long enough, they will win back their losses.

Digital Gambling Machines

Digital gambling machines, such as video poker and slot machines, are becoming increasingly popular and may contribute to addiction.

Prevalence

About 1 percent of the US population is addicted to gambling; an additional 2 to 3 percent are problem gamblers.

Accompanying Disorders

Almost all gambling addicts have another addiction, such as alcoholism, or a mental health or mood disorder.

Costs of Addiction

Gambling addiction causes personal debt, white-collar crime, divorce and family dysfunction, and suicide.

Internet Gambling

To raise tax revenue many states are legalizing or considering legalizing Internet gambling, which is the fastest-growing segment of the gambling industry.

Gambling Addiction and Teens

Teenagers are more vulnerable to gambling addiction because the parts of their brains that control impulses have not matured.

Treatment Options

Twelve-step programs, treatment centers, individual therapy, and medication are used to treat gambling addiction, although some gambling addicts quit without help.

Overview

Shirley gambled for the first time in her mid-twenties, when she and some friends visited Las Vegas. About ten years later, while working as an attorney on the East Coast, she began to visit local casinos. By her late forties she was skipping work four days a week to play blackjack, betting thousands of dollars on each hand. "I wanted to gamble all the time," she told *Scientific American*. "I loved it—I loved that high I felt."[1]

Eventually Shirley was arrested for stealing money from her clients to fund her gambling addiction. After serving two years in prison, she began seeing a therapist to help rebuild her life. At the time, the American Psychiatric Association (APA) did not consider gambling to be addictive, and her counselor never said she was an addict. But after attending Gamblers Anonymous (GA), Shirley concluded that she was addicted to the high she felt at the blackjack table. "It took me a long time to say I was an addict," she says, "but I was, just like any other."[2]

Shirley is one of millions of Americans whose lives have been destroyed by gambling addiction. As it happened in Shirley's case, gambling addiction usually develops slowly over a period of years. Eventually the addicted gambler's life begins to revolve around gambling, making plans to gamble, and getting money with which to gamble. Because most gambling is designed so that the odds favor the house, gambling addicts are destined to lose in the end. Like Shirley, many gamble away everything they own, go into debt, and eventually turn to crime to fund their addiction.

What Is Gambling Addiction?

There is no single authoritative definition of gambling addiction, but because there are so many similarities between gambling and drug addictions, most definitions are modeled after the definition for substance abuse. The Massachusetts Council on Compulsive Gambling defines gambling addiction as "a persistent and recurrent problematic gambling behavior that causes clinically significant distress or impairment in social, occupational, or other important areas of functioning."[3] In other words, gambling addicts have an uncontrollable urge to gamble all the time, despite severe negative consequences or a desire to stop.

> Because most gambling is designed so that the odds favor the house, gambling addicts are destined to lose in the end.

People who are diagnosed with gambling addiction must show at least four of nine symptoms listed in the fifth edition of the *Diagnostic and Statistical Manual of Mental Disorders (DSM-5)*—the key reference book for mental health professionals in the United States and Canada. Again, these criteria are similar to the symptoms for drug addiction. They include a need to gamble more to achieve the same level of excitement, being unable to cut back or stop gambling, and jeopardizing a job or relationship because of gambling.

A Disease with Many Names

Until recently gambling addiction was thought to be a moral failing, not a medical disease. The term *degenerate gambler* (*degenerate* means "immoral") was often used as a slur to express judgment about those who could not control their gambling. Scientists and healthcare professionals used the term *pathological gambling* (*pathological* means "diseased") to describe uncontrolled gambling, and the term first appeared in the *DSM* in 1980. The terms *compulsive gambling* and *disordered gambling* were also widely used, in part because the term *pathological* has negative connotations in popular usage. In 2013, when the fifth revision of the *DSM* was published, the APA changed the term *pathological gambling* to *gambling disorder* and placed it within a new behavioral addictions category. Thus, pathological gambling, compulsive gambling, disordered gambling, and gambling disorder all refer to the same condition, which most people now call gambling addiction.

The term *problem gambler* is sometimes used as a synonym for *gambling addict* in newspapers and magazines. However, scientists use the term to refer to a person who is not yet addicted (does not have four out of the nine symptoms of gambling addiction) but is beginning to experience some of the problems related to gambling and is at risk of developing gambling addiction.

Gambling Takes Many Forms

Gambling is defined as risking something of value—usually money—on a game or event with an unpredictable outcome. It has taken many forms over the centuries, from sports betting in ancient Rome and Greece to stock trading on Wall Street. Most forms of gambling fall into one of two categories: games of chance and games of skill. Games of chance rely on random outcomes. There are different probabilities, or odds, of winning in games of chance. Sometimes it is easy to figure out the odds—a player who calls heads in a coin toss, for instance, has a one-in-two chance of winning. Sometimes, however, knowing the exact odds of winning is more complicated, as it is in blackjack. Other popular games of chance are table games like roulette and craps, slots and other machine games, lotteries and raffles, and bingo.

Games of skill are games in which players can increase their odds of winning by using specialized knowledge or skills. For instance, poker is a game of skill because winning depends upon interpersonal skills such as bluffing effectively. Those without this skill can still enjoy poker as a game of chance, but they will usually lose to a skilled player. Other games of skill include sports betting, bridge, pool or billiards, and stock trading.

Lots of people enjoy an occasional visit to a casino where they can try their luck at blackjack or slot machines. Gambling addicts, on the other hand, have an uncontrollable urge to gamble all the time, regardless of the consequences.

Most people will only gamble on games of skill if there is an element of chance or unpredictability. If one player knows the outcome beforehand, then the game is thought to be unfair.

Gambling addicts often mistake games of chance for games of skill. They sometimes believe they can predict or control the outcome of a game of chance by following their instincts or hitting a button on a slot machine at just the right time. Addicts who enjoy games with complicated odds often believe that they can use their math skills to gain an advantage. However, for a gambling addict, the thrill of risk and uncertainty often overrides any advantage he or she might have.

Why Do People Become Addicted to Gambling?

Before the relationship between behavioral addictions and the brain was well understood, psychologists assumed that the primary motivation for gambling was financial. They thought that people gambled compulsively because they were obsessed with money and striking it rich. However, studies have shown that gambling addicts do not stop gambling after a big win. As one addict explains, "Money became the means to gamble, that's all it was to me."[4]

By studying the brain, researchers discovered that gambling addicts are actually addicted to the heightened state of awareness that gambling produces—a state that is very similar to the heightened state a drug addict experiences. Many gamblers refer to this state as *the zone*—a state of mind in which people can detach from their day-to-day problems and lose themselves in their game of choice. To some—such as people who play table games like blackjack or craps—the zone can be intensely exciting. Others, such as people who enjoy repetitive games like slot machines and video poker, find the zone intensely relaxing. People who have risk factors for gambling addiction, such as having an immediate family member who is addicted to gambling, may find the lure of the zone much more compelling than people who are not at risk. However, many scientists believe that repeated exposure to gambling can intensify the effects of the zone and trigger addiction in almost anyone.

> " Gambling addicts often mistake games of chance for games of skill. "

Though the gambling industry claims that gambling is merely a form of entertainment, casinos do everything they can to encourage players to gamble. The interiors of casinos are designed to help gamblers get into the zone, and casino games are carefully constructed to keep them there. All distractions and interruptions are eliminated. Drinks are free and brought to the players. Even the interruption of collecting a jackpot has been reduced by replacing tokens with plastic cards or paper printouts that can be redeemed at the player's convenience. As one gambling addict explains, "You're not playing for money, you're playing for credit—credit so you can sit there longer, which is the goal. It's not about winning, it's about continuing to play."[5]

> "Casinos do everything they can to encourage players to gamble."

The Expansion of Gambling

In 1976 there were no casinos in the United States outside of Las Vegas, Nevada, and only thirteen states held lotteries. In 2014 gambling is legal in every state but Hawaii and Utah. Gambling on Native American land, known as tribal gaming, was legalized in 1988 and is now a $27 billion industry, with over four hundred casinos in twenty-eight states. Las Vegas is now a family vacation destination dotted with casinos that cost billions of dollars to build. Even Internet gambling is making a comeback after being banned in the United States in 2006. As states struggle with budget shortfalls caused by the recession of 2008, more and more of them are expanding gambling to increase their tax revenue. Between 2009 and 2010, thirty-seven states expanded the types or amount of gambling, mostly by allowing electronic gaming machines (which include slot machines and video poker) to operate in new areas.

The public has had a mixed reaction to the expansion of gambling. Some are happy to have another form of entertainment available to them. Others are concerned that more opportunities to gamble will translate into more addicted gamblers. Addiction specialists are among those who are concerned; of all of the risk factors for gambling addiction, the strongest is having easy access to gambling. Studies have found that the more a person gambles, the more likely he or she is to become addicted. According to Keren Henderson of Stop Predatory Gambling Kentucky, those who live within

10 miles (16 km) of a casino have twice the rate of problem gambling than those who live farther away, and at least half of casino employees—people who are exposed to gambling every day—are problem gamblers. The gambling industry disagrees with these statistics and claims that the rate of gambling addiction has remained steady despite gambling expansion.

Internet Gambling

The fastest-growing segment of the gambling industry is Internet gambling. Although Internet gambling was made illegal in the United States in 2006, the legality of that decision has been argued in the courts, and the federal government has relaxed its enforcement of the ban. This encouraged states like New Jersey to legalize some forms of Internet gambling. Many casinos now have their own Internet gambling websites, including the Tropicana Resort in Atlantic City. However, people may gamble only at the casino websites from inside the state of New Jersey, which the casino confirms by using GPS to locate the player's cell phone.

> **The more a person gambles, the more likely he or she is to become addicted.**

Internet gambling has come under a great deal of criticism because it makes it much easier for teenagers to gamble. According to a study by the Annenberg Public Policy Center, more than half a million high school–aged youths visit a gambling site every month. "Teen problem gambling rates are two to four times the rate of adults," reports the Gambling Disorders Clinic at Columbia University. "Easy access to computers and online gambling take away barriers to gambling."[6] Internet gambling is also similar to other types of online game play that many scientists feel are addictive in their own right. Internet gaming disorder is considered to be a serious addiction in many parts of the world. Many addiction experts worry that the addictive properties of gambling may increase on a medium like the Internet.

Internet Gambling Reinforces the Gambler's Fallacy

Gamblers tend to hold false beliefs and superstitions about gambling. One false belief that is common among both problem and nonproblem

Internet gambling is the fastest-growing segment of the gambling industry. Easy access to online gambling sites has been blamed for a rise in teen gambling and has fueled concerns about gambling addiction.

gamblers is called the gambler's fallacy. The gambler's fallacy is the false belief that, in a game of chance, a win is more likely after a string of losses. For instance, gamblers often believe that a slot machine that has not paid out in a while is more likely to hit a jackpot than one that just hit a jackpot. In actuality, earlier games have no influence on later games; the odds are exactly the same on each play. Many gambling addicts take the gambler's fallacy a step further by believing that if they just keep gambling, their luck will eventually turn around. This is referred to as chasing losses. However, odds at a gambling establishment like a casino are set to favor the house, and the longer a player gambles, the more likely it is that he or she will lose everything.

Some critics of Internet gambling claim that some Internet gambling sites actually reinforce false beliefs with the free versions of their games, also known as simulated gambling. Simulated gambling is popular with young people; in one 2014 Australian study, 30 percent of teens surveyed said they played simulated gambling games. Because simulated gambling is not regulated, the gambling industry is free to manipulate the pattern of wins and losses. Many free games are designed so that the longer a gambler plays, the more he or she wins—the opposite of the design of a typical casino game. As Keith Whyte explains, this practice "may create erroneous expectations for winning that, when the user switches to 'real money' gambling—often hosted or operated by the same company—are extremely dangerous as the longer you play the more likely you are to lose since the odds are now against the user."[7] In other words, simulated gambling can reinforce the false belief that winning big at gambling is easy.

Gambling Machines

The most popular form of gambling today is the gambling machine, which is sometimes referred to as an electronic or digital gaming machine. Gambling machines are often modeled on the mechanical slot machine, though modern gambling machines have video touch screens and contain a computer chip that programs their actions. Gambling machines can offer a wide variety of games of chance, including those with complicated odds like blackjack and poker. In Britain these machines are referred to as fixed-odds betting terminals, or FOBTs (pronounced fob-tees), and they are found in legal sports betting shops. In the United States, depending on a state's laws, gambling machines can be found in casinos, racinos (a combination racetrack and casino), betting shops, restaurants and bars, and even grocery stores.

> " **More than half a million high school–aged youths visit a gambling site every month.** "

Gambling machines are extremely popular with addicted and problem gamblers because they allow for faster play. According to Natasha Dow Schüll, author of *Addiction by Design: Machine Gambling in Las Vegas,* an experienced video poker player can play up to twelve hundred hands per hour. As a representative from Bally's casino explained to Schüll, "A gaming machine is a very fast, money-eating device. The play should take no longer than three and a half seconds per game."[8] Schüll notes that most of the gambling industry's profits come from gambling machines, which are known as "the 'cash cows,' the 'golden geese,' and the 'workhorses' of the industry."[9]

The Prevalence of Gambling Addiction

Most studies show that about 1 percent of the US population, or about 3 million people, are addicted to gambling. Another 2 to 3 percent are considered to be problem gamblers. According to the gambling industry group American Gaming Association (AGA), those percentages have remained relatively steady over the last several decades. However, a comprehensive national study has not been completed by the US government since 1999, when the National Gambling Impact Study Commission report was published. The definition and criteria for gambling addiction has also changed several times since the 1980s, making it difficult to compare figures. For these reasons, it is still unclear whether the expansion of gambling has resulted in an increase in the rate of gambling addiction among the population.

> " Simulated gambling can reinforce the false belief that winning big at gambling is easy. "

Problem gambling and gambling addiction are more prevalent in men than in women, and some experts estimate that men outnumber women approximately five to one. However, because women are less likely to seek treatment for gambling problems, the number of women who are addicted to gambling may be higher. Some experts estimate that one-third of gambling addicts are female. Problem gambling also disproportionately affects teenagers, the poor, and the elderly.

What Are the Costs of Gambling Addiction?

Gambling addiction can have severe costs to individuals, families, and society. Addicts are more likely to abuse drugs and alcohol and have higher rates of depression than the general population. And because they often accumulate huge amounts of debt, many turn to crime to support their gambling addiction—stealing money from relatives, writing bad checks, or embezzling from their workplace.

One reason why the costs of gambling addiction are so severe is that addicts usually do not seek help until they feel they have no other choice.

According to psychiatrist Henrietta Bowden-Jones, by the time gambling addicts come in for treatment, many feel suicidal. Of the patients she treats at her gambling clinic, 18 percent have lost their jobs, 51 percent have lost their partners, and 84 percent have committed illegal acts to support or cover up their habit.

Can Gambling Addiction Be Overcome?

Those who are seeking help with gambling addiction have several options. GA is a 12-step program that is free, confidential, and available in most major cities. Therapy is available through addiction clinics or private psychotherapists, and many therapists can determine whether medication will help with cravings. Many experts believe a combination of therapy, medication, and support from a 12-step program offers the highest chances of success. But recent studies have shown that attempting to cut down or quit gambling without help may be equally effective. Regardless of the method chosen, most gambling addicts relapse several times before they gain control over their addiction.

As ongoing research on behavioral addiction reveals the complex relationship between behaviors and the brain, scientists are working to develop more effective therapies and treatments to bring much needed help to people whose lives have been destroyed by gambling addiction. However, many states are expanding traditional and online gambling opportunities while at the same time cutting their funding for gambling prevention and treatment programs. Experts are concerned that this will increase the incidence of gambling addiction in the future—especially among young people, who are more vulnerable to addiction. They are calling for more insurance companies to cover gambling addiction treatment, especially since the APA has recognized that gambling can be as addictive and destructive as substances like drugs and alcohol. The National Council on Problem Gambling (NCPG) believes that gambling addiction should be included in the behavioral health provisions of the Affordable Care Act. According to the authors of the NCPG's 2014 report on problem gambling and the health care system, "Given that problem gambling has such a profound effect not only on the gamblers and their families but on the entire country, we face both a moral and financial obligation to offer treatment for problem gamblers."[10]

What Is Gambling Addiction?

66 Gambling is the great escape. . . . You escape any pain, any problems, any ambiguities, it's all clear. It's you against fate. 99

—Reverend Thomas Grey, director of the National Coalition Against Gambling Expansion.

66 I've got to understand you can't beat the casino. You might win a lot of money from them, but in the long run they are going to win more money from you. 99

—Former National Basketball Association star Charles Barkley.

When Henrietta Bowden-Jones was working on her doctoral thesis on alcoholism, she administered the Cambridge Gambling Task, a psychological test that would determine which of her subjects were risk takers. In one version of the test, each subject was shown ten squares and told that a token was hidden under one of them. Nine squares were blue and one was red. The subjects were asked to guess which color hid the token. Since it is nine times more likely that the token was under a blue square, most people chose blue.

However, a small percentage of her subjects did the unexpected. "I noticed that some people were predisposed to get highly excited at this," she said, "and press the red one instead." These were the risk takers, the people who were very likely to be addicted to gambling, and Bowden-Jones became intensely curious about them. "I wanted to help them even more than the alcoholics," she explained. "I wanted to know why on earth they were pressing the red."[11]

A Process Addiction

Like all behavioral addictions, gambling addiction is a process addiction. This means that an addicted gambler is not addicted to the goal of gambling, which usually is to win money. Instead, the gambler is addicted to the process of gambling—the preparation, the sights and sounds in the environment, the physical actions that accompany the game, and the thrill of taking a risk and anticipating a win. For instance, people who are addicted to playing the lottery (a common form of gambling in which the player risks the cost of a ticket to win a larger sum) will not stop gambling if they win a jackpot. They will continue to crave the process of looking forward to the nightly drawing, checking their numbers against those that are drawn, and experiencing a rush of excitement if some of their numbers match.

> People who are addicted to playing the lottery will not stop gambling if they win a jackpot.

When gamblers are gambling, their senses are heightened, their problems are forgotten, and they are intensely focused on the task at hand. Money becomes a means to keep the experience of gambling going, and winning simply means that that experience can be extended a little longer. Mollie, a Las Vegas resident who is addicted to video poker machines, explains the experience:

> In the beginning there was excitement about winning, but the more I gambled, the wiser I got about my chances. Wiser, but also weaker, less able to stop. Today when I win—and I do win, from time to time—I just put it back in the machines. The thing people never understand is that I'm not playing to win. [I play] to keep playing.[12]

Risk Factors

Anyone can become addicted to gambling. However, researchers have found that some characteristics are more common in gambling addicts than in the general population. These characteristics are sometimes called risk factors because those who exhibit them are more at risk for developing gambling addiction. Most of these risk factors do not directly cause a person to become addicted to gambling. For instance, some studies have shown that teenagers who play sports are more likely to become gambling addicts. This does not mean that playing sports causes gambling addiction or that quitting sports in any way reduces the risk of becoming a gambling addict. It simply means that people who enjoy playing sports also tend to enjoy gambling and are therefore more likely to eventually become addicted to gambling.

Having a highly competitive personality, being a risk taker, being impulsive, and being restless or easily bored are all traits commonly seen in gambling addicts. Researchers have found that having one or more of these traits as a child puts a person at risk of becoming an addict later in life. A 2012 study that tracked almost a thousand individuals over thirty years found that three-year-olds who had traits such as restlessness, willfulness, and impulsiveness were more than twice as likely to become addicted to gambling as adults. "Perhaps it is the combination of impulsivity (or risk taking) in conjunction with the tendency toward negative emotions, such as anger, hostility, and anxiety, that constitutes the personality vulnerability for disordered gambling [gambling addiction],"[13] the authors of the study speculate.

> " Gambling during the teenage years . . . puts young people at risk for developing gambling addiction later in life. "

Gambling during the teenage years, or being in a family environment that condones gambling, also puts young people at risk for developing gambling addiction later in life, as does having an unstable home life or experiencing childhood trauma. Having a mood disorder like depression or another addiction like alcoholism is also a risk factor. For instance, a 2014 Danish study found that adults who were problem gamblers were 2.7 times more likely to be heavy smokers and 2.2 times more likely to be heavy drinkers than those who were not problem gamblers.

An Inherited Addiction

Scientists have found that there is a strong genetic component to gambling addiction. For instance, one study of Australian twins published in

JAMA Psychiatry found that it was more likely for identical twins to both be addicted to gambling than it was for fraternal twins. Because identical twins have the same genetic makeup, these results indicate that genetics play a part in gambling addiction.

Other studies have shown that individuals who have a parent or a grandparent who gambles heavily or is addicted to gambling are more likely to become addicted themselves. While scientists still are not sure exactly how many gambling addicts have gambling addiction in their families, Bowden-Jones, who founded Britain's National Problem Gambling Clinic (NPGC), says that about 30 percent of her patients have parents or grandparents who are also gambling addicts. Other researchers say about half of all gambling addicts have relatives who gamble.

The Poor and the Elderly Are at Risk

Some groups are more vulnerable to developing problem gambling and gambling addiction than others. For instance, gambling addiction tends to be more prevalent in people who live in poverty. Many studies have found that poor populations spend a greater percentage of their income on gambling than wealthier populations, and low-income gamblers are more likely to have gambling-related problems, including financial difficulties. According to Casino-Free Philadelphia, an organization that wants to remove casinos from that city, one study found that those living in the most impoverished areas of New York State spent eight times more of their income on lottery tickets than did those living in the most affluent sections. And a 2013 study by the Research Institute on Addictions (RIA) at the University at Buffalo, State University of New York, found that problem gambling was more than twice as prevalent in neighborhoods with the highest levels of poverty compared to neighborhoods with the lowest levels of poverty. Furthermore, within the poorest neighborhoods, the individuals with the lowest socioeconomic status had the greatest risk of developing gambling

> " **Individuals who have a parent or a grandparent who gambles heavily or is addicted to gambling are more likely to become addicted.** "

addiction. RIA senior researcher John W. Welte speculates that this may be because there are few role models of financial success in disadvantaged neighborhoods. "Gambling may be viewed as one of the few opportunities for financial advancement," he says, "and perhaps provides the lure as a means for easily gaining money."[14]

Lower-income senior citizens are especially vulnerable to problem gambling and gambling addiction. Casinos regularly market free day trips to seniors that include transportation to and from the casino and vouchers for free meals and gambling. This gives a population that often feels cut off from society an opportunity for what the AGA calls "an inexpensive day out for someone on a fixed income."[15] Dennis McNeilly, a psychologist who specializes in issues that affect the elderly, notes that "casinos regularly send mailings and even birthday cards. If you're isolated or lonely, that matters."[16] All of these factors make casinos attractive to seniors, particularly those who do not have many options for recreation.

> **Lower-income senior citizens are especially vulnerable to problem gambling and gambling addiction.**

Teenage Gambling

Teens and young adults have the highest rates of problem gambling. Of young adults aged fourteen to twenty-one, 2.1 percent struggle with problem gambling and another 6.5 percent are at risk. According to KnowTheOdds.org, the New York Council on Problem Gambling's educational website, "Gambling at the ages of 10 or 11 can seem innocent and harmless, but studies have shown that children who are introduced to and begin gambling by age 12 are four times more likely to become problem gamblers."[17] Despite the fact that gambling is illegal for young people, almost 80 percent of twelve-year-olds report having engaged in some form of gambling for money.

One reason is that teenagers tend to exhibit more problems with impulse control than adults. This is because the prefrontal cortex—the area of the brain responsible for complex thought and impulse control—does not fully mature until the age of twenty-five. According to the US Department of Health and Human Services, "With an immature prefrontal cortex, even if teens understand that something is dangerous, they may still go ahead and engage in the risky behavior."[18] Scientists also think that the teenage brain is more vulnerable to addiction because it is still developing.

Young people also are more susceptible to gambling addiction because a big win makes a big impression on them. Their reasoning skills are not yet mature, so they tend to believe that winning is easy. Arnie Wexler became addicted to gambling when he was a young teenager. As a child, he was insecure; "the only time I felt okay about myself was after I had a win," he explains. Then, when he was fourteen, he went to the racetrack for the first time and won fifty-four dollars. "Looking back today, I think it was that night that changed my life. Even though it was only $54, it was about five weeks' salary to me at that time. That night gave me the belief that I could be a winner from gambling and eventually become a millionaire. I can still recall that high feeling walking out of the racetrack."[19]

Many young people are introduced to the concept of gambling with online gambling simulation games. Even nongambling online games encourage competition and drive players to keep playing until they advance a level or win a game. Experts believe the excitement and competition of these games primes young people for machine and Internet gambling later in life. While Internet gamblers (like casino gamblers) must be twenty-one to legally gamble, many teens manage to bypass age restrictions to gamble online. Because of this, teens are at risk more than ever before of developing gambling problems before they reach adulthood. And like adults, they run the same risk of incurring large amounts of debt or turning to crime to fund their addiction.

Warning Signs

Gambling addiction usually happens gradually, which is another reason why it is easy for the gambler to hide it. However, experts say that family members and close friends should look for the warning signs of problem gambling and gambling addiction. For instance, new secrecy over finances, or a new desire to control household finances, might mean that a gambler is trying to hide losses. Missing valuables, dwindling savings, or overdue bills may mean that a gambler is losing control of the ability to stop gambling. Asking friends and family for money, unexplained loans, or increased credit card debt may mean that a gambler is trying to chase losses. Finally, criminal activity like stealing from relatives, writing bad checks, stealing money from work, or committing insurance fraud may be signs of gambling addiction.

Even if gambling addiction is spotted early by a family member or loved one, most gambling addicts do not seek help until they are out of options. For this reason, experts believe that the more education young people receive about the dangers of gambling, the better chance they will have to avoid becoming addicted.

Primary Source Quotes*

What Is Gambling Addiction?

66 **Unlike most casual gamblers who stop when losing or set a loss limit, compulsive gamblers are compelled to keep playing to recover their money—a pattern that becomes increasingly destructive over time.** 99

—Mayo Clinic, "Compulsive Gambling: Symptoms," February 12, 2014. www.mayoclinic.org.

The Mayo Clinic is one of the top-rated hospitals in the United States.

66 **Problem gamblers experience intense excitement, power and hopeful anticipation as a result of the 'action' of gambling.** 99

—Massachusetts Council on Compulsive Gambling, "Gambling Disorders and Substance Abuse Disorders," March 5, 2014. www.masscompulsivegambling.org.

The Massachusetts Council on Compulsive Gambling is a private, nonprofit health agency dedicated to reducing the costs of gambling disorders.

Bracketed quotes indicate conflicting positions.

* Editor's Note: While the definition of a primary source can be narrowly or broadly defined, for the purposes of Compact Research, a primary source consists of: 1) results of original research presented by an organization or researcher; 2) eyewitness accounts of events, personal experience, or work experience; 3) first-person editorials offering pundits' opinions; 4) government officials presenting political plans and/or policies; 5) representatives of organizations presenting testimony or policy.

Primary Source Quotes

 28

❝Most individuals who regularly gamble will at some point experience the hallmark features of problem gambling behavior—namely, difficulty controlling time and money spent on the activity, with negative consequences.❞

—Natasha Dow Schüll, *Addiction by Design: Machine Gambling in Las Vegas.* Princeton, NJ: Princeton University Press, 2012. Kindle edition.

Schüll is a cultural anthropologist and a professor at the Massachusetts Institute of Technology (MIT).

❝Pathological gamblers don't have track marks on their arms. They are not walking around with an unsteady gait. They don't have signs of liver cirrhosis. They're not shaking when they're talking to you.❞

—Henrietta Bowden-Jones, in TEDMED Live Royal Albert Hall, "Treating Addiction Against All Odds: Henrietta Bowden-Jones at TEDMEDLive Imperial College 2013," YouTube video, May 21, 2013. www.youtube.com.

Bowden-Jones is a psychiatrist, neuroscience researcher, and founder of the NPGC in the United Kingdom.

❝Any initial pleasure in winning can contribute to a desire to win *more*—and that is where the problem gambling cycle begins for many people.❞

—KnowTheOdds.org, "Problem Gambling: When Winning Doesn't Make You Stronger," July 9, 2014. http://knowtheodds.org.

KnowTheOdds.org is an educational website created by the New York Council on Problem Gambling (NYCPG).

❝[The] combination of having experienced little control, lots of chaos and too little genuine caring during childhood (even if there were lots of false displays of it), can make a building with no windows and lots of machines and tables where you might get 'lucky' feel like home.❞

—Keith Ablow, "The Psychology of Compulsive Gambling," Fox News, January 5, 2012. www.foxnews.com.

Ablow is a psychiatrist and member of the Fox News medical information team.

❝Gambling is not a free-market business. Unlike most businesses in the US, legalized gambling is mainly the product of government laws, which determine the types of gambling that is permitted, the number, location, and size of establishments allowed, and so forth.❞

—AddictionBlog.org, "Top 10 Gambling Facts," May 29, 2011. http://gambling.addictionblog.org.

AddictionBlog.org is a website dedicated to connecting people struggling with addiction with appropriate treatment options.

❝[Gambling] addicts do not handle boredom well and they often do not know how to fill free time other than with their addiction.❞

—Brad Girtz, "Residential Treatment for Gambling Addiction: 5 Things to Look For," AddictionBlog.org, September 27, 2013. http://gambling.addictionblog.org.

Girtz is an executive at Life Works, a residential treatment center for addictions in the United Kingdom.

❝The current generation of youth will spend their entire lives with gambling easily accessible, readily available, and state-owned and/or regulated.❞

—Jeffrey Derevensky, et al., eds., *Youth Gambling: The Hidden Addiction.* Boston: Walter de Gruyter, 2011, p. 5.

Derevensky is a professor at McGill University in Canada and is the cofounder of the International Centre for Youth Gambling Problems and High-Risk Behaviors.

What Is Gambling Addiction?

- The AGA estimates that about **1 percent** of the US population, or **3.2 million people**, meet the criteria for gambling addiction.

- The NCPG reports that **75 percent** of Americans over the **age of 13** gambled in 2012.

- According to *Scientific American,* **4 out of 5 Americans** say they have gambled at least once in their lives.

- With the exception of Utah and Hawaii, every state in the United States has some form of legalized gambling.

- Gambling disorder is the only behavioral addiction described in the *DSM-5*.

- According to Georgia State University, about **50 percent** of gambling addicts commit crimes.

- According to the British national daily newspaper the *Guardian*, in 2014 there were **2,691 betting shops** in the poorest **55 boroughs** in England, which is **2 times** more than in the richest **115 boroughs**.

- A document leaked to the *Guardian* showed that in April 2013, the equivalent of more than **$1.6 billion** was bet on FOBTs in England.

Diagnostic Criteria for Gambling Disorder

In the fifth revision of the *Diagnostic and Statistical Manual for Mental Disorders (DSM-5)*, Pathological Gambling was renamed Gambling Disorder and reclassified a behavioral addiction. In order for a person to be diagnosed with a gambling disorder, he or she must exhibit four or more of the symptoms below over a twelve-month period.

- Needs to gamble with increasing amounts of money in order to achieve the desired excitement
- Is restless or irritable when attempting to cut down or stop gambling
- Has made repeated unsuccessful efforts to control, cut back, or stop gambling
- Is often preoccupied with gambling (e.g., having persistent thoughts of reliving past gambling experiences, handicapping or planning the next venture, thinking of ways to get money with which to gamble)
- Often gambles when feeling distressed (e.g., helpless, guilty, anxious, depressed)
- After losing money gambling, often returns another day to get even ("chasing" one's losses)
- Lies to conceal the extent of involvement with gambling
- Has jeopardized or lost a significant relationship, job, or educational career opportunity because of gambling
- Relies on others to provide money to relieve desperate financial situations caused by gambling

Source: Problem Gambling Institute of Ontario, "DSM-5 Diagnostic Criteria: Gambling Disorder," 2014. www.problemgambling.ca.

- According to a 2013 Japanese Health Ministry Survey, **4.8 percent** of the population in Japan, or **5.36 million** people, are addicted to gambling.

- A 2013 study published in the *American Journal on Addictions* found that US veterans were **2 times** more likely to be addicted to gambling than are members of the general population. Those with a history of substance abuse were **3 times** more likely, and those with mood disorders were **2.5 times** more likely.

Gambling Is Widespread Among Teens

Studies of Canadian teens show that, while teen substance abuse increas
dramatically as they get older, gambling may be even more common from
early age. By the seventh grade most are involved in gambling, and their
involvement stays steady through eleventh grade. This trend is worrisome
because most studies of adults who are either problem gamblers or addic
find that they began gambling for money between the ages of ten and twe
For these studies, gambling was defined as wagering money on the outcc
of any uncertain event, such as the result of a card game or a sporting ev

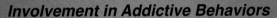

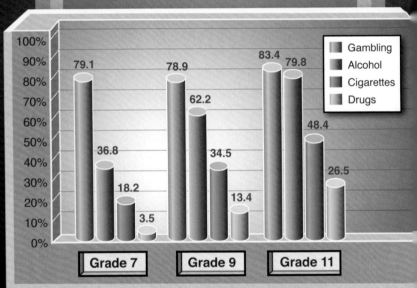

Involvement in Addictive Behaviors

Source: Jeffrey L. Derevensky, *Teen Gambling: Understanding a Growing Epidemic* (Kindle edition).
Plymouth, UK: Rowman & Littlefield, 2012.

- A 2014 Australian survey of students **aged 12 to 17** found that **percent** had participated in simulated gambling on the Internet.

- According to the NCPG, social casino games are the fastest-growi segment of the gambling industry, with an estimated **170 mill monthly users** and revenues of approximately **$2 billion** in 2012.

Toddlers' Temperaments Predict Gambling Addiction Later in Life

Three-year-olds who had undercontrolled temperaments were more than twice as likely to be addicted to gambling as adults than were three-year-olds with well-adjusted temperaments. (A child with an undercontrolled temperament was described in the study as showing a combination of being restless, willful, impulsive, withdrawn, and negative, among other characteristics.) Researcher Wendy Slutske discovered this when she analyzed temperament data on three-year-olds who had been followed since birth in the Dunedin Study, a general health and development study of the lives of 1,037 babies born in New Zealand between 1972 and 1973 that is now in its fifth decade. Slutske's research confirms that some personality types are more vulnerable to gambling addiction than others are.

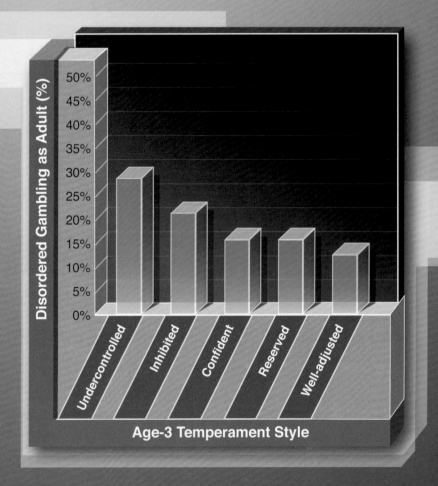

Source: *Psychological Science*, "Undercontrolled Temperament at Age 3 Predicts Disordered Gambling at Age 32: A Longitudinal Study of a Complete Birth Cohort," Wendy S. Slutske et al., May 14, 2012, p. 513.

Why Do People Become Addicted to Gambling?

66The more legalized gambling a state makes available, the more pathological behavior is triggered.99

—Bernard P. Horn, political director of the National Coalition Against Legalized Gambling.

66Despite the dramatic expansion of gaming across the country in recent years, the prevalence rate of pathological gambling has remained relatively unchanged.99

—American Gaming Association, the US gaming industry association.

W hile some people are more likely to become addicted to gambling than others, the development of addiction—the process of moving through the stages of casual gambler to problem gambler to addicted gambler—is not well understood. The gambling industry claims that addiction is a brain disease caused by a combination of genetics and other factors that originate in the mind of the addict—not in the activity of gambling. As proof of this, the AGA cites statistics that show that even though gambling has expanded dramatically since the 1980s, the prevalence rate of problem gambling and gambling addiction is about the same. "If casinos and slot machines cause increased gambling addiction, we would see a corresponding increase in gambling problems with the expansion of casino gambling across the country,"[20] the AGA states on its website.

However, many addiction experts disagree with this argument. They believe that it is meaningless to talk about the percentage of gambling addicts among the general population because only a part of that population is regularly exposed to gambling. As Schüll explains, "The percentage of pathological and problem gamblers among the gambling population is a good deal higher [than 1 percent], and higher still among regular (or 'repeat') gamblers—20 percent, by some estimates."[21] In addition, many people who do not fit the criteria for gambling addiction still can experience some of the same problems as addicts, such as having trouble controlling how much time and money they spend on gambling. Researchers like Schüll believe that if such a high percentage of gamblers are addicts, and if nonaddicts can behave like addicts some of the time, then there must be something about gambling itself, or about the way gambling is presented and manipulated by the gambling industry, that causes addiction in vulnerable individuals. In other words, they believe that, just like substance addiction, gambling addiction is caused by two factors: an individual's propensity for addiction and the addictive qualities of gambling itself.

> "There must be something about gambling itself, or about the way gambling is presented and manipulated by the gambling industry, that causes addiction in vulnerable individuals.

Gambling Creates Addiction in Vulnerable Brains

Addiction is a physical process that affects the brain's pleasure center, one of the oldest structures in the brain. The pleasure center is part of a reward system that encourages people to do things that help them to survive. Brain chemicals like dopamine provide that encouragement by creating a feeling of anticipation, heightened attention, and pleasure. New connections between the regions of the brain that control memory, movement, and motivation are formed, changing the structure of the brain so that the activity will be easier to do in the future.

The brain is designed so that natural activities such as eating or having sex trigger the release of dopamine and other pleasure chemicals. However, sometimes the reward system gets hijacked by substances that do not contribute to survival, such as drugs. A drug like cocaine makes the brain release up to ten times the amount of dopamine than it normally does, which is why cocaine is considered to be highly addictive.

Scientists used to believe that only drugs could cause addictions, but they are now finding that behaviors can be addictive as well. "The past idea was that you needed to ingest a drug that changes neurochemistry in the brain to get addicted, but we now know that just about anything we do alters the brain," says Timothy Fong, a professor of psychiatry at the University of California, Los Angeles (UCLA), and director of UCLA's Addiction Medicine Clinic. "It makes sense that some highly rewarding behaviors, like gambling, can cause dramatic changes, too."[22]

Recent research into gambling addiction has shown that drugs and gambling alter the brain's circuits in very similar ways. For instance, if the brain is exposed to gambling over a long period of time, several things happen. First, the brain protects itself from the constant flood of dopamine by shutting down some of its dopamine receptors. Once this happens, a gambler no longer gets the same rush from gambling and has to take more risks or make larger bets to get the same pleasurable feeling. This process is called tolerance, and studies have shown that it works the same way in the brains of drug addicts and addicted gamblers.

> " Gambling addicts do not quit when they are losing because their brains are unable to make rational decisions while they are gambling. "

Drugs and gambling also change the structure of the brain in the same way. Both cause neural pathways that connect the reward system to the prefrontal cortex—the center for rationality in the human brain that helps us control impulses—to become weaker. Therefore, the longer a person is exposed to an addictive substance or behavior, the more impulsive he or she becomes. A 2012 study in Amsterdam found that when addicts were gambling, the electrical activity in the prefrontal cortex was significantly reduced in areas that help people assess risks and suppress urges. In other words, gambling addicts do not quit when they are losing because their brains are unable to make rational decisions while they are gambling.

High on Gambling: The Zone

Most people find gambling—and winning—to be fun. When people gamble, they enter into a heightened state of anticipation known as the zone, which many find pleasurable. For some gamblers, the zone is a highly focused, trance-like state that is at once fun, relaxing, invigorating, and satisfying. At first this state is punctuated by bursts of pleasure brought on by winning. After a while, however, the brain adapts, tolerance sets in, and winning ceases to be a pleasurable rush unless the risk is increased.

> **Up to 85 percent of a casino's revenue in the United States comes from gambling machines.**

For the gambling addict, entering the zone, rather than winning, becomes the point of gambling. Many addicted gamblers say that they can escape from pain, anxiety, or responsibility while in the zone. As one gambling machine addict explains, "It's like being in the eye of a storm. . . . Your vision is clear on the machine in front of you but the whole world is spinning around you, and you can't really hear anything. You aren't really there—you're with the machine."[23] Studies have shown that the more time a person spends in the zone, the more the brain is changed and the stronger addiction becomes.

Casinos Encourage Players to Get into the Zone

Because repeat players bring in 30 to 60 percent of a casino's revenue, the industry has carefully studied what these repeat customers want. According to former casino game designer Gardner Grout, "Our best customers are not interested in entertainment—they want to be totally absorbed, they want to get into a rhythm."[24] In other words, they want to enter the zone.

Because up to 85 percent of a casino's revenue in the United States comes from gambling machines, every detail of a casino's design is constructed to get—and keep—machine gamblers in the zone. For instance, every part of the typical modern casino, from the lighting, the sound level, the width of the aisles, the ceiling height, and the carpet pattern is designed to draw attention to gambling machines. The casino itself is laid out in a maze, with gambling machines prominently displayed at every turn. According to Bill Friedman, a casino manager and former gambling addict whose theories of casino design revolutionized the industry, "If a visitor has a propensity to gamble, the maze layout will evoke it."[25]

The placement and construction of the gambling machines themselves are also designed to give gamblers a feeling of being comfortably enclosed in their private world. Some machines are covered with a false roof or overhang; others, like Bally's trademarked Privacy Zone cabinets, have recessed screens and partitions between players. Machine seating and consoles are also designed to be as comfortable as possible. In fact, in 2005 a presentation on gambling machine design at the gambling industry's annual convention was titled "Building a Better Mousetrap: The Science of Ergonomics." As one machine design consultant explained, "The key is duration of play. I want to keep you there as long as humanly possible—that's the whole trick, that's what makes you lose."[26]

Gambling Machines May Accelerate Addiction

As Keren Henderson of Stop Predatory Gambling Kentucky explains, "Slot machines [are] engineered to create fast, continuous, repeat betting that industry insiders call 'playing to extinction.' Simply put, slot machines are designed to keep players in their seats until they run out of money."[27] For instance, most gambling machines include technology that replaces coins and tokens with paper tickets, which may make money seem more abstract to the player and therefore easier to risk. Another innovation, called Powercash, allows players to transfer funds from their checking accounts and credit cards to their player cards right at the gambling machine or, in jurisdictions where this is illegal, from a modified ATM machine at the end of each row of gambling machines. Nancy, a nurse who eventually went bankrupt because of her gambling addiction, claims it is this easy access to cash that accelerated her addiction. "I used to bring cash with me [to the casino], and when it was gone I'd have no choice: I'd have to leave. That all changed with the ATMs." On one occasion, Nancy lost her entire bank account balance in six hours. "My car payment, my insurance payment, my rent—I lost everything. I went back and forth between the ATM and the machine about four or five times in one night; it took me about five hours to lose it all. I played myself to death, right down to the nickel slots."[28]

Not only are gambling machines designed to keep players gambling until they run out of money, they may be more addictive than other types of gambling. Studies have shown that modern gambling machines are more addictive than other types of gambling. Robert Breen, a psychiatrist from Brown University, found that individuals who play gambling machines become addicted to gambling three to four times faster than those who play cards or bet on sports. Schüll explains that the reason for this is that modern gambling machines are so fast that games can be completed every few seconds with no pause in between them, which speeds the progression of the addiction. "Some machine gamblers become so caught up in the rhythm of play that it dampens their awareness of space, time and monetary value,"[29] Schüll writes in the *New York Times*. According to psychologist Mark Dickerson, this effect of the modern gambling machine "erodes the player's ability to maintain a sequence of informed and rational choices about purchasing the next game offered,"[30] which is another hallmark of gambling addiction.

Gambling Machines May Encourage Superstition

Gambling addicts tend to be superstitious and hold many false beliefs about gambling—beliefs that contribute to their addiction. For instance, gambling addicts often believe that certain objects or rituals bring luck or that wins are rewards and losses are punishment for previous behavior. Many gambling addicts also experienced a big win when they first started gambling, which made them believe that gambling was easy. At the heart of all of these false beliefs is the idea that they have more control over the outcome of their game of choice than they actually do.

> " Modern gambling machines are so fast that games can be completed every few seconds with no pause in between them. "

Schüll and others are concerned that gambling machines reinforce—and in some cases create—these false beliefs. For instance, many gambling machines give a player the ability to push a button to stop the spinning of a slot machine wheel, which gives players the impression that they have some control over where the wheel stops. In reality, the outcome of a game on a modern gambling machine is decided as soon as a player begins a round of play, and the spinning wheels are simply computer simulations. This false sense of control can encourage gambling addicts to bet heavier and play longer than they would if they believed the outcome of play was truly random.

Despite a growing body of evidence, the gambling industry denies that gambling or modern gambling machines encourage or create addiction. According to Christine Reilly, executive director of the gambling industry–funded Institute for Research on Pathological Gambling and Related Disorders, "Things are not addictive, they're just not. . . . I play a slot machine for 10 minutes and I'm so bored I want to shoot myself. If you don't have [the] vulnerability, the odds are you won't get addicted."[31] However, a growing body of evidence supports the idea that the very techniques the industry uses to keep players gambling may be addicting the most vulnerable among them.

> " The gambling industry denies that gambling or modern gambling machines encourage or create addiction. "

Primary Source Quotes*

Why Do People Become Addicted to Gambling?

Primary Source Quotes

> **The casinos' real money comes from a smaller number of problem gamblers who show up day after day.**

—Keren Henderson, "Gambling Preys on the Poor," Cincinnati.com, March 22, 2014. www.cincinnati.com.

Henderson is the executive director of Stop Predatory Gambling Kentucky.

> **The small percentage of the population that does not gamble responsibly—estimated at about 1 percent—is not the main source of revenue for gaming establishments.**

—American Gaming Association, "Are Pathological Gamblers the Main Source of Revenue for Casinos?," 2014. www.americangaming.org.

The AGA is the US gambling industry association.

Bracketed quotes indicate conflicting positions.

* Editor's Note: While the definition of a primary source can be narrowly or broadly defined, for the purposes of Compact Research, a primary source consists of: 1) results of original research presented by an organization or researcher; 2) eyewitness accounts of events, personal experience, or work experience; 3) first-person editorials offering pundits' opinions; 4) government officials presenting political plans and/or policies; 5) representatives of organizations presenting testimony or policy.

❝Just as certain individuals are more vulnerable to addiction than others, it is also the case that some objects . . . are more likely than others to trigger or accelerate an addiction.❞

—Natasha Dow Schüll, *Addiction by Design: Machine Gambling in Las Vegas.* Princeton, NJ: Princeton University Press, 2012. Kindle edition.

Schüll is a cultural anthropologist and a professor at MIT.

❝*Why* people continue to gamble is not always about winning money—and winning a significant amount of money on a bet does not make the problem gambler ready to stop gambling.❞

—KnowTheOdds.org, "Problem Gambling: When Winning Doesn't Make You Stronger," July 9, 2014. http://knowtheodds.org.

KnowTheOdds.org is an educational website created by the NYCPG.

❝When compared to the general population, a significant body of evidence shows that veterans . . . are at greater risk for and have a higher prevalence of problem gambling.❞

—Raanan Kagan et al., *Problem Gambling in the 21st Century Healthcare System*, National Council on Problem Gambling, July 3, 2014. www.ncpgambling.org.

Raanan Kagan is a behavioral health consultant for Carnevale Associates, which offers research services to public policy organizations.

❝On rare occasions, gambling becomes a problem with the very first wager. But more often, a gambling problem progresses over time. In fact, many people spend years enjoying social gambling without any problems. But more frequent gambling or life stresses can turn casual gambling into something much more serious.❞

—Mayo Clinic, "Compulsive Gambling: Symptoms," February 12, 2014. www.mayoclinic.org.

The Mayo Clinic is one of the top-rated hospitals in the United States.

> **❝Machine gambling is associated with the greatest harm to gamblers.❞**

—Natasha Dow Schüll, *Addiction by Design: Machine Gambling in Las Vegas.* Princeton, NJ: Princeton University Press, 2012. Kindle edition.

Schüll is a cultural anthropologist and a professor at MIT.

> **❝[Simulated] gambling-like sites may condition or habituate youth to gambling, making them more likely to engage in 'real money' gambling and/or develop gambling problems.❞**

—Keith Whyte, letter to the Senate Subcommittee on Consumer Protection, Product Safety & Insurance, National Council on Problem Gambling, July 12, 2013. www.ncpgambling.org.

Whyte is the executive director of the NCPG.

> **❝Some people mistakenly believe that almost winning means an actual win can't be too far behind or that their chances must be improving. Neither belief is correct.❞**

—Addictions Foundation of Manitoba, "Near Miss Beliefs: Close Doesn't Count," GetGamblingFacts.ca, 2014. http://getgamblingfacts.ca.

The Addictions Foundation of Manitoba is a Canadian agency that provides addiction services throughout the province of Manitoba.

Facts and Illustrations

Why Do People Become Addicted to Gambling?

- The Yale University's Center of Excellence in Gambling Research analyzed data about **2,006 Connecticut high school student gamblers** and found that problem gambling was more common in adolescents who gambled online versus those who did not participate in Internet gambling.

- According to the NCPG, **40 percent** of Internet gambling sites surveyed inflated their payout rates (over **100 percent** return) in the free demo version of their games, which can mislead players into thinking that winning is easier than it actually is.

- According to addiction expert Schüll, people who regularly play video gambling devices become addicted **3 to 4 times** more quickly than other gamblers.

- A 2011 report produced by the National Centre for Social Research found that in England the gambling industry had placed more FOBTs in poorer areas than in more wealthy areas, a fact that the industry had denied.

- A 2013 study published in the *Journal of Behavioral Addictions* found that more than **11 percent** of people in the poorest US neighborhoods were problem gamblers, as compared to **5 percent** in the wealthiest neighborhoods.

Gambling Affects Different Parts of the Brain

The illustration below shows the main sections of the brain involved in pleasure and addiction. Dopamine is the main chemical involved in gambling addiction. When the brain experiences unexpected results—such as the rewards in gambling—dopamine activates the pleasure circuit.

Brain Sections Involved in Gambling

The strongest pleasures are produced by the largest rewards, and these occur in a number of regions of the pleasure circuit and structures interconnected with the pleasure circuit.

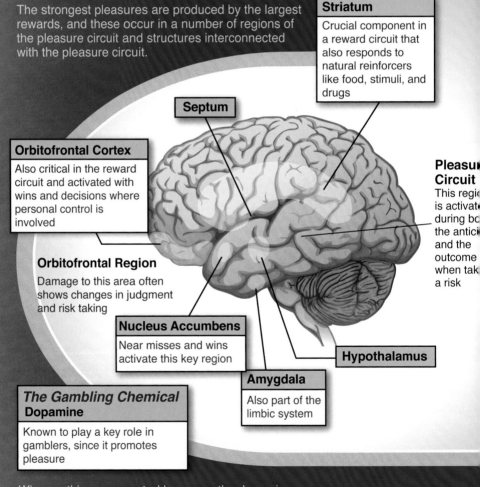

Striatum
Crucial component in a reward circuit that also responds to natural reinforcers like food, stimuli, and drugs

Septum

Orbitofrontal Cortex
Also critical in the reward circuit and activated with wins and decisions where personal control is involved

Pleasure Circuit
This region is activated during both the anticipation and the outcome when taking a risk

Orbitofrontal Region
Damage to this area often shows changes in judgment and risk taking

Nucleus Accumbens
Near misses and wins activate this key region

Hypothalamus

Amygdala
Also part of the limbic system

The Gambling Chemical
Dopamine
Known to play a key role in gamblers, since it promotes pleasure

When nothing unexpected happens, the dopamine system is quiet, but when needed the dopamine signal is sent to a higher region of the brain, the frontal cortex.

Source: Diego Martinez-Moncada, "The Psychology of Gambling," Daily Infographic, July 18, 2012.
http://dailyinfographic.com.

Londoners Believe Gambling Machines Are Addictive

The Campaign for Fairer Gambling interviewed five hundred people as they exited betting shops in London after playing fixed-odds betting terminals (FOBTs), which are electronic gambling machines that allow gamblers to play casino games like roulette or poker. Most of those surveyed had spent more money than planned or gambled all of their money on FOBTs—two behaviors associated with addiction. The vast majority surveyed believed FOBTs cause addictive behavior.

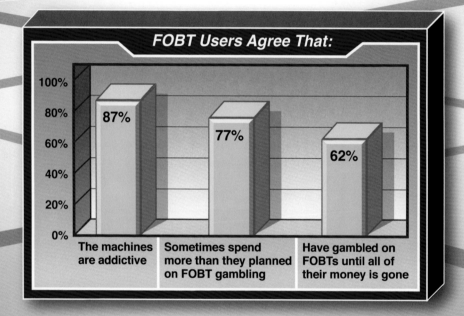

FOBT Users Agree That:

The machines are addictive	87%
Sometimes spend more than they planned on FOBT gambling	77%
Have gambled on FOBTs until all of their money is gone	62%

Source: Campaign for Fairer Gambling, "FOBT Research Report," June 18, 2013. http://fairergambling.org.

- To make it easier for residents to gamble, Las Vegas's neighborhood casinos offer easy parking, child-care facilities, and other amenities.

- A study titled "Effects of Ambient Odors on Slot-Machine Usage in a Las Vegas Casino" found that slot revenue rose by a full **45 percent** in a gambling area that was subtly treated with a pleasing odor.

Gambling in a Casino Atmosphere Encourages Rapid and Impulsive Play Style

A study of nonproblem gamblers found that those who gambled in a simulated casino setting did not slow their play after a loss and made decisions faster than those who gambled in a lab setting that had no resemblance to a casino. This indicates that casino atmospheres encourage rapid and potentially impulsive decision making—styles of play associated with addiction.

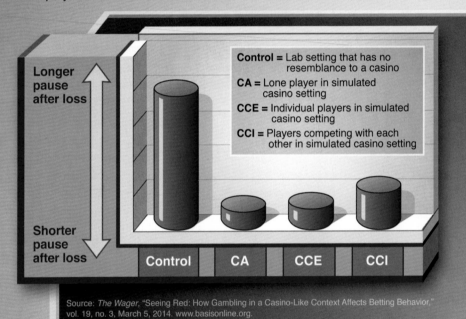

Longer pause after loss

Shorter pause after loss

Control = Lab setting that has no resemblance to a casino

CA = Lone player in simulated casino setting

CCE = Individual players in simulated casino setting

CCI = Players competing with each other in simulated casino setting

| Control | CA | CCE | CCI |

Source: *The Wager*, "Seeing Red: How Gambling in a Casino-Like Context Affects Betting Behavior," vol. 19, no. 3, March 5, 2014. www.basisonline.org.

- According to Casino-Free Philadelphia, when video lottery machines were temporarily shut down in South Dakota, gambling treatment centers in South Dakota saw their telephone inquiries drop from **68 per month to 0**.

- Gaming machine designers have added various features to slot machines, such as television monitors and bingo ticket printers, to encourage players to stay seated at their gambling machine and continue playing.

What Are the Costs of Gambling Addiction?

> **"The expansion of legalized gambling destroys individuals, wrecks families, increases crime, and ultimately costs society far more than the government makes."**
>
> —Bernard P. Horn, political director of the National Coalition Against Legalized Gambling.

> **"The preponderance of evidence demonstrates that the social problems in communities with casinos are no different than those in communities without casinos."**
>
> —American Gaming Association, the US gaming industry association.

In 2009 Justyn Rees Larcombe was a successful director of a financial services company in the United Kingdom. A former officer in the British army, he had a family, a nice house, and a healthy savings account. Then he got a taste of gambling by placing a small bet online on a rugby match. By 2013 he had gambled away his savings and the equity in his house and was using his company credit card to fund his gambling. At one point he even sold a precious heirloom—a ceremonial sword—that he had planned to leave to his sons. "I cried when I left the antique shop, because it hurt doing that," he tells the British Broadcasting Corporation. "But I spent the £200 [$324] within probably two hours that afternoon."[32]

Larcombe managed to pay off his debts and turn his life around, but countless others do not. They lose their families and their freedom, and they sometimes take their own lives. The damage they cause is rarely confined to themselves. Studies show that as many as ten people are directly harmed by the actions of each addicted gambler, and gambling addiction costs the United States $6 billion to $7 billion each year.

Losing Control and Racking Up Debt

As addiction takes over, a gambler's judgment begins to deteriorate until he or she can no longer make wise financial decisions. Like a person under the influence of drugs or alcohol, an addicted gambler loses the ability to control impulses. The desire to continue gambling begins to take over the addict's life; he or she will sacrifice everything to keep gambling, placing bet after bet until every cent has been lost. "I found myself homeless, no money, no job. I cashed in my pension," explains Simon, a recovering addict who was addicted to gambling at FOBTs in UK betting shops. "They caused me to lose everything."[33]

> "As addiction takes over, a gambler's judgment begins to deteriorate."

Gambling addicts accumulate enormous amounts of debt. According to the financial information website Debt.org, the average gambling addict generates between $55,000 and $92,000 worth of debt before seeking treatment. More than 20 percent are forced to file for bankruptcy because of gambling losses. Gambling addicts deplete their savings, borrow against their homes and their belongings, and borrow from friends and family. Ninety percent withdraw cash advances from their credit cards—debt that typically has a very high interest rate. They also borrow from casinos. Most casinos grant loans to customers while they are gambling, either by extending credit at a gambling table or loading funds directly onto a player card at a gambling machine. In fact, Debt.org states that only about half of the money spent in casinos is brought in by players—the rest is borrowed from the casino.

Guilt and Shame

Gambling addicts usually feel a great deal of guilt and shame about their debt, especially if it affects their spouse. Debt is the reason that addicts lie to their friends and family and hide their gambling habit. Bobby Gee, who regularly took money from his workplace to pay his mortgage, says that lying got to be a way of life. "I got so good at lying. The things I was saying I actually started to believe myself," he says. "To this day [my wife] doesn't know how bad it was."[34]

Shame is usually what prevents gambling addicts from seeking treatment until they have no other option. Unfortunately, many addicts have lost everything by the time they admit their addiction. Bowden-Jones says that most of those who seek help from her clinic "have no job, and no contact with friends because they've tried to borrow money and people have disowned them. They have no spouse, they've lost touch with their parents [and] they have no home."[35]

Families Destroyed

Any type of financial strain puts stress on a relationship, but an addicted gambler's debt is particularly damaging, especially to marriages. Because gambling addicts tend to hide their behavior for as long as possible, their spouses are often taken by surprise by the financial damage. They learn after the fact that their life savings have been lost or that they are responsible for debt that their spouse has accumulated. And even when the addicted spouse recovers from the addiction, the debt remains—sometimes for life. The strain of this can cause marital discord, violence in the household, and divorce. The divorce rate among gambling addicts is twice that of the general population, and Las Vegas has the highest divorce rate in the nation.

> " Shame is usually what prevents gambling addicts from seeking treatment until they have no other option. "

Philip Mawer, author of *Overcoming Gambling*, says that when his wife finally realized how much he had lost gambling, she attacked him with a kitchen knife. Mawer's wife later died of complications of alcoholism, but he blames her death on his gambling, which he says exacerbated her drinking. "She simply couldn't come to terms with all the wasted years we'd had together and what and where we could have been, had it not been for my gambling,"[36] he writes on his blog.

White-Collar Crime

Studies have shown that about half of all gambling addicts break the law because of their addiction. Most commit what is known as white-collar crime; in fact, the American Insurance Institute estimates that 40 percent of all white-collar crime is committed by gambling addicts. They write bad checks, embezzle money from their workplaces, steal from family members, sell prescriptions, shoplift, and commit insurance fraud to finance their gambling or pay off gambling debts. The more serious an addict's gambling problem, the more likely he or she is to steal. One study by the New Jersey Institute for Problem Gambling found that out of four hundred GA members, 57 percent stole a total of $30 million.

> " Between 17 and 20 percent of all addicted gamblers attempt suicide. "

Whereas some gambling addicts use crime to fund their addiction, others see crime as the only way they can salvage their lives and get out of debt. Unfortunately, many gamble with the money they steal, hoping to win a jackpot. Marilyn Lancelot, author of *Gripped by Gambling,* tried to get out of debt by stealing from her employer. Each time she forged her boss's name on a check, she believed she would win enough to pay everything back before she was discovered. Five years later she was arrested and sentenced to two years in prison for embezzling $300,000.

Suicide

The most devastating result of gambling addiction is suicide. Studies have shown that between 17 and 20 percent of all addicted gamblers attempt suicide—twenty times the rate of the general population. About half of all gambling addicts who are in treatment have suicidal ideation, or obsessive thoughts about suicide. The spouses of addicted gamblers are also at risk for suicide. For many, in the face of what seems to be insurmountable debt, suicide seems to be the only way out. As Bowden-Smith explains, "So many pathological gamblers experience suicidal ideation . . . because they feel trapped in a reality that they have not chosen for themselves."[37]

Las Vegas has the reputation for being the suicide capital of America. At one time, people in Las Vegas (residents and visitors) had a 50 percent higher risk of suicide than people living elsewhere in the country. In recent years, however, Las Vegas has dropped to having the fifth-highest suicide rate. "As more states legalize casinos, more and more gamblers are committing suicide across the country,"[38] writes Paul Davies, a journalist who edits the blog *Get Government Out of Gambling*. For instance, in the two years after a casino opened in Gulfport, Mississippi, suicides increased 213 percent. And in the first year after casinos opened in Biloxi, Mississippi, suicides increased 1,100 percent.

The Cost to Society

One of the biggest arguments against the expansion of gambling is that when a casino opens in a community, crime goes up and social welfare generally suffers. Studies show that most localities see a rise in crime, bankruptcy, and foreclosure. This is most evident in Las Vegas, where two-thirds of the residents gamble, many on a regular basis. According to Politifact.com, Nevada is number one in underemployment in the nation, number two in violent crime, and number three in robberies and car theft.

The main reason for the expansion of gambling is that states are hoping to shore up their budgets by taxing gambling revenue. Yet according to Davies, the costs associated with crime and social problems puts even more financial strain on already depleted state budgets. "[This raises] the question of why lawmakers would enable public policies that harm citizens when they take an oath to protect them,"[39] Davies writes. Casino-Free Philadelphia explains that the increase in crime and cost of associated police, court, and prison costs can offset much of the tax revenue casinos provide. According to economist Earl Grinols, gambling addicts who turn to crime can cost communities between $20,500 and $45,700 per year.

Problems for Young and Old Gamblers

Young people who are problem gamblers often disconnect from family, peers, and school because they are focusing on gambling games. As their debt mounts, they can become overwhelmed by stress and guilt, especially since they have withdrawn from their support system. In college, when most young adults get their first credit card, their opportunities to gamble increase, and their debt accumulates. And because most believe that addiction is an adult issue, they put off getting help until they can no longer hide their addiction. The debt college gamblers accumulate can follow them for the rest of their lives.

Problem gambling can be especially problematic for seniors because they tend to be on fixed incomes. Brian Kongsvik, the help-line director for the Florida Council on Compulsive Gambling in Sanford, Florida, notes that people in the over-fifty population are usually unable to make back the money they have lost. They are sometimes forced to rely on their children, which Kongsvik says can lead to depression, illegal activities like stealing or writing bad checks, and even suicide. Although there are no recent national studies of the prevalence of gambling problems among older Americans, Kongsvik says that "twenty-five percent of the calls we receive for help each month come from someone 55 years or older or from a worried loved one calling about a relative in that age group."[40]

> **Gambling addicts usually do not seek help until they are overwhelmed by debt or in trouble with the law.**

The Hidden Addiction

One reason why the costs of gambling addiction are so high is that the addict is able to hide his or her addiction for such a long time. This is why gambling addiction is often referred to as the hidden addiction. According to Ron Turrell, a counselor at the addiction charity Norcas, "The big difference between gambling and alcohol and drugs is that it's much easier to hide."[41] Because there are no physical symptoms of gambling addiction, addicts usually only need to hide their financial losses and make excuses about the time they spend gambling. This means that gambling addicts usually do not seek help until they are overwhelmed by debt or in trouble with the law. By this time, many have been addicted for years.

Mawer says that when he was hiding his addiction, his wife did not suspect he was gambling—instead, she thought he was spending up to nine hours a day online because he was having an affair. Mawer was able to hide his addiction for years before his wife realized the extent of the financial damage to their family. He estimates that over twenty years he lost the equivalent of about $830,000.

For many people gambling is an enjoyable pastime that never becomes an addiction. But for a small percentage of the population, gambling is an addiction and, like many addictions, it can have serious consequences. Gambling addiction comes with a high cost—it can burden families and ruin lives.

What Are the Costs of Gambling Addiction?

—Sam Magavern, "Another Voice: Expanding Casino Gambling Will Hurt More than Help," *The Buffalo News*, October 31, 2013. www.buffalonews.com.

Magavern is the codirector of the Partnership for the Public Good, a community advocacy organization in Buffalo, New York.

❝Casinos are crime magnets with two types of illegal activity: Internal corruption that includes money laundering, loan sharking and mob influence, and street crime.❞

—Kerri Toloczko, "As Native American Casinos Proliferate, the Social Costs of the Gambling Boom Are Ignored," *Forbes*, September 25, 2013. www.forbes.com.

Toloczko is a Senior Fellow with Let Freedom Ring, a conservative public policy organization.

Bracketed quotes indicate conflicting positions.

* Editor's Note: While the definition of a primary source can be narrowly or broadly defined, for the purposes of Compact Research, a primary source consists of: 1) results of original research presented by an organization or researcher; 2) eyewitness accounts of events, personal experience, or work experience; 3) first-person editorials offering pundits' opinions; 4) government officials presenting political plans and/or policies; 5) representatives of organizations presenting testimony or policy.

66 Not only do some people who develop gambling disorder literally gamble away everything they own, and end up in crippling debt, but far more of them become suicidal than would be expected in the general population. 99

—Elizabeth Hartney, "What Is Gambling Disorder?," About Health, September 27, 2013. http://addictions.about.com.

Hartney is a psychologist who specializes in addictions and concurrent disorders.

66 [Casinos] don't just provide jobs; these are quality jobs. Our industry has a proven track record of hiring locally, providing jobs with upward mobility, and committing to a diverse work force. 99

—Frank J. Fahrenkopf, "Casino Jobs Are Good Jobs," Baltimore Sun, October 31, 2012. http://articles.baltimoresun.com.

Fahrenkopf is the president and CEO of the American Gaming Association.

66 So long as card clubs and casinos, and their executives, obey the rules, they should not be legally responsible for the harm compulsive gamblers do to themselves. 99

—I. Nelson Rose, "Compulsive Gambler Just Can't Win," Gambling and the Law, 2011. www.gamblingandthelaw.com.

Rose is a lawyer and one of the world's leading experts on gambling law.

66 Problem gambling has a large social cost related to lost productivity and work disruption, unemployment, family breakdown, mental and physiological health problems, legal and financial difficulties, crime, bankruptcy, and suicide. 99

—Sally Gainsbury, Internet Gambling: Current Research Findings and Implications. New York: Springer Science, 2012, p. 41.

Gainsbury is a clinical psychologist at the Centre for Gambling Education and Research at Southern Cross University, Australia.

"Most gambling addicts are in serious financial trouble and they often have no idea how to handle finances or stick to a budget."

—Brad Girtz, "Residential Treatment for Gambling Addiction: 5 Things to Look For," AddictionBlog.org, September 27, 2013. http://gambling.addictionblog.org.

Girtz is an executive at Life Works, a residential treatment center for addictions in the United Kingdom.

....

"I've left bills unpaid, sometimes for weeks, months, or years. I've had credit cards canceled and had creditors harass me with phone calls at all hours, sometimes leaving me screaming at the walls."

—Sam Skolnik, *High Stakes: The Rising Cost of America's Gambling Addiction.* Boston: Beacon, 2011. Kindle edition.

Skolnik is an award-winning journalist who writes about gambling addiction.

....

"If you knew casino operators, slot machine makers and the politicians they partner with don't use slot machines or gamble, why would you allow them to target your family and the citizens of your community, luring them to gamble away their savings, often turning their lives totally upside down?"

—Les Bernal, "Why Don't Casino Advocates and Executives Patronize Casinos?," *New Hampshire Union Leader,* March 11, 2014. www.unionleader.com.

Les Bernal is the national director of Stop Predatory Gambling, which is based in Washington, DC.

....

Facts and Illustrations

What Are the Costs of Gambling Addiction?

- The NCPG estimates that the bankruptcies, burglaries, spouse abuse, child neglect, foreclosures, and even suicide associated with gambling addiction costs the United States between **$6 billion and $7 billion** each year.

- The American Insurance Institute estimates that **40 percent** of all white-collar crime (such as embezzlement, insurance fraud, etc.) is committed by or for compulsive gamblers.

- **One out of 5 gambling addicts** attempts suicide.

- According to the American Insurance Institute, gambling addicts are responsible for an estimated **$1.3 billion** worth of insurance fraud per year.

- The NCPG estimates that gambling addicts cost American businesses **$40 billion** in lost wages and insurance claims each year.

- A 2011 study of US adults published in *Psychiatry Research* found that those who gamble in more than one setting experience poorer general health than those who gamble in only one setting.

- A 2014 Danish study published in the *Journal of Gambling Studies* found that adults who were problem gamblers were **2.7 times** more likely to be heavy smokers and **2.2 times** more likely to be heavy drinkers than those who were not problem gamblers.

Study Links Problem Gambling with Family Violence

In a 2013 Australian study of 1,030 people who were seeking help with problem gambling in their families, 52 percent reported family violence. Participants in this group were then asked two questions: "In the past twelve months, have you physically hurt, insulted or talked down to, threatened with harm, or screamed or cursed at a family member?" and "In the past 12 months, has a family member physically hurt you, insulted or talked down to you, threatened you with harm, or screamed or cursed at you?" The study illustrated that there is a high co-occurrence of problem gambling and family violence.

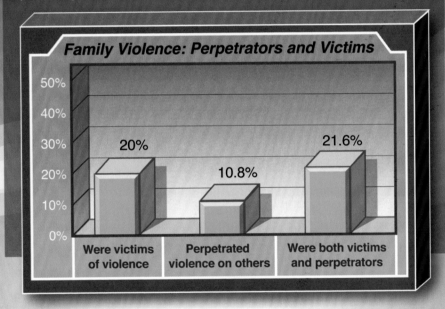

Family Violence: Perpetrators and Victims

- Were victims of violence: 20%
- Perpetrated violence on others: 10.8%
- Were both victims and perpetrators: 21.6%

Source: *Asian Journal of Gambling Issues and Public Health*, Aino Suomi, et al. "Problem Gambling and Family Violence: Family Member Reports of Prevalence, Family Impacts and Family Coping," 2013, p.13.

- According to the Responsible Gambling Council of Ontario, as problem gambling severity increases, so does the likelihood of having a psychological disorder, especially antisocial personality disorder, panic disorder, major depression, and phobias.

- **One out of 3 prison inmates** meets the criteria for gambling addiction.

US Gamblers Lose the Most

The international newspaper the *Economist* reported that in 2013, the United States led the world in the amount of money lost to gambling. Gambling is also getting to be more popular worldwide—losses in 2013 were the highest on record.

US — $119
China — $76
Japan — $31.4
Italy — $23.9
Britain — $19.9
Australia — $18.4
Germany — $14.8
France — $13.3
Canada — $13
Spain — $12.4

Americans Lose $119 Billion Through Gambling
Biggest gambling losses by country in 2013 (in billion US dollars)

Source: Mathias Brandt, "Americans Lose 119 Billion Through Gambling," Statista, February 6, 2014. www.statista.com.

- A 2013 Swedish study found that adults who were close to problem gamblers (spouses, children, friends, etc.) suffered from more work, debt, and legal problems and had more physical and mental health difficulties than the general population.

- According to KnowTheOdds.org, gambling addiction has the highest suicide rate of all addictions.

- According to Georgia State University, gambling addicts are imprisoned at nearly **2 times** the rate of problem gamblers and nearly **6 times** the rate of low-risk gamblers.

Can Gambling Addiction Be Overcome?

66With an annual social cost of approximately $7 billion, coverage for the prevention and treatment of gambling addiction is clearly the most ethical and economical way to minimize harm.99

—Keith Whyte, executive director of the NCPG.

66[At the GA meeting] everyone present has bounced a check, faced bankruptcy, and at least contemplated suicide. . . . A few proclaim that gambling is harder to kick than heroin and crack.99

—Bill Lee, author of *Born to Lose: Memoirs of a Compulsive Gambler*.

Most experts estimate that only about 5 percent of addicted gamblers seek formal treatment. For those who do, there are several different options available: 12-step programs, therapy, and even medication. The choice of treatment depends upon an individual's preferences, needs, and, perhaps most importantly, whether he or she has any other addictions. According to Brad Girtz of Life Works, a residential treatment center in the United Kingdom that treats gambling and other addictions, "If all the addictions are not addressed, addicts often slip back into their old behavior and end back in the cycle of [gambling] addiction."[42]

However, most people do not seek out formal treatment and choose to quit gambling on their own. The reasons for this are unclear, but some experts believe it is because gambling addiction is still thought of as a weakness or moral failing, and addicts may be too embarrassed to admit to the problem. Bowden-Jones notes that the average financial loss experienced by gamblers who come to her UK clinic for help is the equivalent of about $243,000. "To turn up at the clinic and say 'I want to repay this money, help me with money management' takes a lot of courage,"[43] she explains.

Gamblers Anonymous

The most popular treatment program is GA, a 12-step program modeled on Alcoholics Anonymous (AA). GA is a self-supporting fellowship group founded in September 1957 in Los Angeles, California. GA adopts the twelve steps and other features of AA, including sharing one's experiences with addiction with the group. Bill Lee, a recovering gambling addict and the author of *Born to Lose: Memoirs of a Compulsive Gambler*, believes that the sharing portion of the typical GA meeting is extremely therapeutic for first-time visitors, who typically have run out of options and are filled with shame and self-hatred. As established members share their stories of addiction, new members learn that their experiences are not unique. This lessens their shame and allows them to start on the road to recovery.

> " The average financial loss experienced by gamblers who come to one UK clinic for help is the equivalent of about $243,000. "

There are over seventeen hundred GA groups in the United States and about three hundred in Canada. In addition, groups are active in eighty-six international cities. Spouses and family members can attend Gam-Anon meetings, available in forty states, to learn how to support addicts and to share ideas of how to cope with the financial consequences of addiction.

Even though GA is a popular first step for gambling addicts seeking help with their addiction, the failure rate of GA is high. Most experts believe that about 90 percent of GA members relapse and return to gambling at least once.

Therapy and Counseling

Many psychologists, therapists, and counselors specialize in addiction issues and can assist gambling addicts with psychological issues related to their addiction. The NCPG is one of many organizations that offer training and certification to addiction counselors who wish to treat gambling addiction. Since addicts often must deal with issues of anger, depression, and shame related to their addiction, a qualified therapist is sometimes necessary to help manage these powerful feelings. In addition, most therapists work in conjunction with a psychiatrist who can assess an addict's mental status and offer medication to alleviate some of his or her symptoms.

Therapists use several different strategies when treating gambling addiction. Motivational interviewing is a technique commonly used with addicts who are seeking therapy to appease a spouse or loved one but who are not yet ready to give up gambling entirely. With this technique, the therapist helps the addict evaluate his or her addiction with the aim to provoke an internal motivation to change. Behavioral therapy is another technique in which the therapist helps the addict put into practice ways to avoid triggers, manage cravings, and deal with relapses. In addition, addicts who have experienced childhood trauma often find it useful to examine those experiences with a therapist and assess how they are contributing to the addiction.

> " Medications can be effective in reducing an addict's urges to gamble. "

Many experts believe that the most effective style of therapy for dealing with gambling addiction is cognitive behavior therapy (CBT). In CBT the therapist works with the addict to develop strategies to replace or avoid problematic thoughts. Patients undergoing CBT are often asked to write down and analyze their thoughts, identifying those that are exaggerated or false beliefs. The CBT-based program that Bowden-Jones uses at the NPGC boasts an 80 percent success rate. "The focus is very much on . . . getting people to modify their behaviors; replacing the negative with positive things that enhance their lives and fill the void left by gambling," Bowden-Jones explains. "It tends to work, even with people who are very unwell with other conditions—depression, anxiety, schizophrenia."[44]

Medication

Because gambling addiction is similar to substance addiction, medications can be effective in reducing an addict's urges to gamble. For instance, drugs called opiate antagonists can be effective in reducing cravings. Opiate antagonists chemically block the pleasurable feelings that are created by gambling or substance use. People who take opiate antagonists usually notice that gambling is no longer as pleasurable, which helps them resist urges to gamble. Antidepressants are also sometimes used to correct a suspected dopamine imbalance that can contribute to addiction. However, antidepressants can provoke a manic episode in a person who is bipolar. Since people who experience manic episodes often act out by gambling, physicians must be careful about prescribing antidepressants to people with problem gambling issues.

According to addiction psychiatrists Sanju George and Henrietta Bowden-Jones, many gambling addicts who are experiencing depression, anxiety, or other physical or mental health problems are unaware that these are actually symptoms of their addiction. Unfortunately, their family doctor may be equally unaware. "Due to low awareness among health professionals about problem gambling," George and Bowden-Jones write, "symptoms [such as depression] are often treated on face value, resulting in the underlying addiction remaining hidden and ignored."[45] Gambling addiction cannot be treated by medication alone, and doctors who only treat the symptoms of gambling addiction risk complicating the problem for their patients.

A Combination Approach

Many experts believe that the best treatment programs combine therapy, medication, and attendance in a 12-step program. UCLA psychiatrist and addiction expert Timothy Fong believes that all three approaches are required for successful recovery. He explains:

> We work with a bio-psycho-social model. First we look at medications that can curb the desire to gamble. If someone acts out because of depression then an antidepressant is most likely going to help with that particular problem behavior. Secondly, we address the psychological component of the disease. Through CBT (Cognitive Behavioral

Therapy), supportive therapies and motivational interviewing, we can help the addict re-learn how to live. And
thirdly, we advocate for the social piece through 12 step
programs and network building.[46]

Fong's program focuses on the four dimensions that support recovery,
as defined by the Substance Abuse and Mental Health Services Administration (SAMHSA). They are health, home, purpose, and community.
According to the SAMHSA model, recovery is most successful when
a person is "physically and emotionally healthy," has "a stable and safe
place to live," has "meaningful daily activities," and has "relationships
and social networks that provide support, friendship, love, and hope."[47]
Fong believes that gambling addicts have the best chance for a successful
recovery in programs that employ this model.

Going It Alone

The idea that gambling addicts must undergo formal treatment—prefer-
ably a combination treatment approach—has been questioned by some researchers. One study published in the *American Journal of Psychiatry* found
that 36 to 39 percent of individuals who had a history of gambling addiction had not experienced any symptoms of gambling addiction in the year
leading up to the study. However, only 7 to 12 percent of them had sought
out counseling or attended Gamblers Anonymous meetings to help to
overcome their addiction. This suggests that many people can and do stop
gambling on their own without the help of a formal treatment program.

Many gambling addicts attempt to stop gambling—or at least to mini-
mize the effects of gambling on their lives—by self-regulation. This technique can be effective in slowing down the progression to addiction in problem gamblers. Some people limit the type of gambling they participate in to
reduce their financial risk. Others limit their exposure to opportunities to
gamble. Sam Skolnik, the author of *High Stakes: The Rising Cost of America's
Gambling Addiction,* claims that he has been addicted to poker since 2001.
Because he does not want to quit, he is thinking about trying a technique
he read about in the memoirs of two gambling addicts. "Neither ended up
in recovery," he writes. "Instead, both say their answer has been to limit
their gambling to a weekly poker game with friends at reasonable stakes."
Skolnik quotes one of the gamblers as saying that this solution "'shows me

that I'm no longer out of control, fighting a dragon I could never slay.'"[48]

Other gambling addicts use a method of limiting exposure to gambling called self-exclusion. Self-exclusion is a process by which gamblers voluntarily ask a casino or other gambling venue to ban them from gambling. They agree to be arrested for trespassing if they are caught gambling. For instance, in a one-year period, seventy-three people who had signed self-exclusion agreements with Ohio's casinos were later charged with criminal trespassing.

Most self-exclusion agreements are legally binding, but they are not well enforced. "It's completely up to the individual to police themselves," explains Scott Anderson of the Ohio Bureau of Problem Gambling. "Unless they run into someone at the casino who knows them or they win a jackpot or use their player card, they would go undetected."[49] Players who gamble anyway and win a jackpot

> **Self-exclusion is a process by which gamblers voluntarily ask a casino or other gambling venue to ban them from gambling.**

are not entitled to their winnings, but many gamble anyway. Since the Illinois self-exclusion program began in 2002, casinos have confiscated $1.5 million of winnings. Casinos legally cannot keep confiscated winnings. Instead, they are used to fund gambling addiction programs.

Financial Counseling

Finally, financial counseling is an important part of recovery for gambling addicts, regardless of whether they seek help in a formal program or try to quit gambling on their own. The debt that gambling addicts accumulate can be a source of intense stress and shame, which can push them to try to eliminate their debt by gambling again. Most casinos have programs in place to help gambling addicts pay their debt over time. Credit counseling services are also useful to gambling addicts who have run up considerable credit card debt.

Casinos Help Out

The gambling industry funds most of the research into gambling addiction in the United States. They have repeatedly denied that they deliberately exploit problem gamblers or intentionally contribute to gambling addiction. "Casinos make money by entertaining people and making sure they have an enjoyable experience," the AGA states on its website. "They have no desire to take advantage of individuals with psychological disorders or problems."[50]

Many casinos actively try to spot gambling addicts and offer them assistance. Whereas some help addicts into intense treatments, others simply offer them information. "There is a strong belief among many of the casino executives that there is a moral obligation to do this," says Alan Feldman, a vice president at MGM Resorts International and chair of the National Center for Responsible Gaming (NCRG). "But there's also a strong business reason: Problem gamblers make for lousy customers. By their very nature, they will turn into bad debt. For them to hit bottom, they have to cause a lot of pain along the way, to themselves, their families, and to companies. It serves no purpose in any business to have customers who can't pay their bills."[51]

> " Many casinos actively try to spot gambling addicts and offer them assistance. "

According to Donald Weinbaum, executive director of the Council on Compulsive Gambling of New Jersey (CCGNJ), there are a few signs that a casino patron may be having problems with addiction. "If you have a regular patron and you see them making larger, crazy wagers, it might be that they're trying to break even," he explains. "It might be that they're caught up in an addiction. If you see a patron going through mood swings, that could be another indication."[52] Most states require gambling establishments to have some form of program in place to help problem gamblers, even if it is simply posting information about where to get help. But many do more. When John Conklin, vice president of player development at Resorts Casino Hotel in Atlantic City, learned that a couple had lost $205,000 to five Atlantic City casinos, he reached out to Arnie Wexler, the former head of the CCGNJ, for help. Wexler now trains casino workers to spot problem gamblers. He got the couple into a program for gambling addicts and helped them work out a payment plan with the casinos.

Recovery Is Possible

Most experts agree that the key to recovering from gambling addiction is to seek help as early as possible. Some gambling addicts are able to educate themselves about their addiction and beat it on their own, but others need the help of a 12-step program or an addiction specialist. Regardless of the treatment method chosen, gambling addicts should not be discouraged if they relapse. According to Bowden-Jones, to beat gambling addiction for good, "being an optimist is very very helpful. . . . I know many people who have been abstinent for decades, for whom it took six, seven, eight times before they got it right."[53]

Can Gambling Addiction Be Overcome?

❝If our teenagers' problem gambling isn't halted early, it can have devastating consequences that affect the rest of their lives.❞

—KnowTheOdds.org, *The Dangers of Youth Gambling Addiction,* May 2013. PDF e-book. http://knowtheodds.org.

KnowTheOdds.org is an educational website created by the NYCPG.

....

❝If problem gamblers are bailed out, they don't have to face the financial problems and can continue to gamble, adding to future problems.❞

—Addictions Foundation of Manitoba, "Near Miss Beliefs: Close Doesn't Count," 2014. http://getgamblingfacts.ca.

The Addictions Foundation of Manitoba is a Canadian agency that provides addiction services throughout the province of Manitoba.

....

Bracketed quotes indicate conflicting positions.

* Editor's Note: While the definition of a primary source can be narrowly or broadly defined, for the purposes of Compact Research, a primary source consists of: 1) results of original research presented by an organization or researcher; 2) eyewitness accounts of events, personal experience, or work experience; 3) first-person editorials offering pundits' opinions; 4) government officials presenting political plans and/or policies; 5) representatives of organizations presenting testimony or policy.

66 Breaking the cycle of compulsive gambling . . . requires resolving to no longer be complicit in their own destruction. It means realizing that the people and places they thought embraced them, were actually shaking them down. 99

—Keith Ablow, "The Psychology of Compulsive Gambling," Fox News, January 5, 2012. www.foxnews.com.

Ablow is a psychiatrist and member of the Fox News medical information team.

66 Treatment and research resources should target adolescents in need. Early interventions can help ensure that today's adolescents do not become tomorrow's adult problem gamblers. 99

—Raanan Kagan et al., *Problem Gambling in the 21st Century Healthcare System*, National Council on Problem Gambling, July 3, 2014. www.ncpgambling.org.

Kagan is a behavioral health consultant for Carnevale Associates, which offers research services to public-policy organizations.

66 Some compulsive gamblers may have remission where they gamble less or not at all for a period of time. However, without treatment, the remission usually isn't permanent. 99

—Mayo Clinic, "Compulsive Gambling: Symptoms," February 12, 2014. www.mayoclinic.org.

The Mayo Clinic is one of the top-rated hospitals in the United States.

66 Most states do not have adequate public health or consumer protection programs in place to address current gambling problems, let alone expanded internet gambling. 99

—Keith Whyte, letter to the Senate Subcommittee on Consumer Protection, Product Safety & Insurance, National Council on Problem Gambling, July 12, 2013. www.ncpgambling.org.

Whyte is the executive director of the NCPG.

❝Often treatment centers are prepared to treat alcohol and drug addiction, but they may not have the rules and procedures in place to properly treat someone suffering from a gambling problem.❞

—Brad Girtz, "Residential Treatment for Gambling Addiction: 5 Things to Look For," AddictionBlog.org, September 27, 2013. http://gambling.addictionblog.org.

Girtz is an executive at Life Works, a residential treatment center for addictions in the United Kingdom.

❝It is essential that public health workers develop primary and secondary prevention programs that can help young people avoid or limit [gambling] addiction.❞

—Howard J. Shaffer, in Jeffrey Derevensky, et al., eds., *Youth Gambling: The Hidden Addiction.* Boston: Walter de Gruyter, 2011, p. xii.

Shaffer is the director of the Division on Addiction at Harvard Medical School.

❝We must educate our kids about the potential dangers of gambling in an effort to prevent future gambling addiction.❞

—KnowTheOdds.org, *The Dangers of Youth Gambling Addiction,* May 2013. PDF e-book. http://knowtheodds.org.

KnowTheOdds.org is an educational website created by the NYCPG.

❝As more states are seeking to expand gambling, legislators at the same time are taking less responsibility for the problem and pathological gamblers they've helped to create.❞

—Sam Skolnik, *High Stakes: The Rising Cost of America's Gambling Addiction.* Boston: Beacon, 2011. Kindle edition.

Skolnik is an award-winning journalist who writes about gambling addiction.

Can Gambling Addiction Be Overcome?

- There are no medications currently approved by the Food and Drug Administration for the treatment of gambling addiction.

- Antidepressants are sometimes prescribed to treat gambling addiction, but they can also trigger a manic episode in people with bipolar disorder, which can cause compulsive gambling.

- According to the AGA, **12 states** require casinos to adopt and carry out responsible gaming policies as a condition of getting licensed. They include Nevada, Louisiana, Iowa, Mississippi, Pennsylvania, Florida, Illinois, and New York. New Jersey has no such requirement for its Atlantic City casinos.

- According to the AGA, many states assess a charge on casinos to help fund treatment programs for gambling addicts.

- In Arizona **97 percent** of those who completed treatment reported reduced participation in gambling activity.

- Oregon's treatment program reported a **40 percent** drop in suicidal ideation, a **75 percent** decrease in illegal acts, and a **73.6 percent** rate of abstinence from gambling **1 year** after treatment.

- A University of Nevada, Las Vegas, study of **75 gamblers** who sought treatment at one of Nevada's state-sponsored problem gambling programs found that **91 percent** reported reduced gambling frequency during treatment and **66 percent** reported abstinence from gambling.

Little Money Spent on Fighting Gambling Addiction

States and nonprofits (including nonprofits funded by the gambling industry) spend approximately $60 million each year to fight gambling addiction. This amount represents 0.1 percent of the 2012 legal gambling revenue of $95 billion.

$95 Billion
Total gambling revenue in 2012

$60 million
Amount spent fighting gambling addiction in 2012

Source: Kevin Whyte, Letter to the Senate Subcommittee on Consumer Protection, Product Safety & Insurance. National Council on Problem Gambling, July 12, 2013. http://www.ncpgambling.org.

- Gambling Therapy, a website run by a residential treatment program for addicted gamblers in the United Kingdom, is one of many websites that offer online support for gambling addicts and their families.

- In 2008, after losing nearly **$1 million**, Arelia Taveras sued one Las Vegas casino and six Atlantic City casinos for **$20 million**, claiming that they had a responsibility to recognize her gambling addiction and cut her off. The lawsuit was dismissed.

- According to the NCPG, among those who seek treatment, **75 percent** drop out of the programs they are steered to, and only **50 percent** of those who remain end up quitting gambling.

Gambling Addicts Favor Abstinence and Willpower

The Massachusetts Council on Compulsive Gambling asked people who are probably addicted to gambling to rate different treatment options for gambling addiction. The people in this group rated abstinence and willpower as the most effective treatment options and Gamblers Anonymous as the least effective treatment option. In contrast, a separate questionnaire given to nongamblers rated family support, professional treatment, and Gamblers Anonymous as the most effective options.

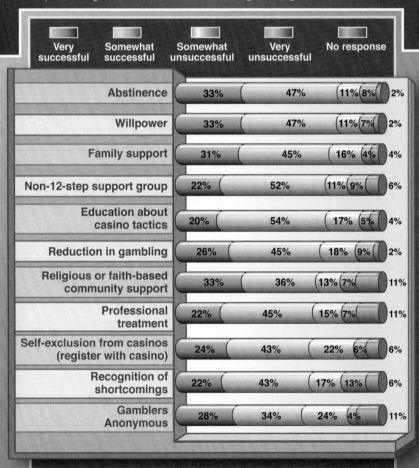

Probable Pathological Gamblers

How successful do you feel each solution tends to be in helping problem gamblers recover from their gambling disorder?

	Very successful	Somewhat successful	Somewhat unsuccessful	Very unsuccessful	No response
Abstinence	33%	47%	11%	8%	2%
Willpower	33%	47%	11%	7%	2%
Family support	31%	45%	16%	4%	4%
Non-12-step support group	22%	52%	11%	9%	6%
Education about casino tactics	20%	54%	17%	5%	4%
Reduction in gambling	26%	45%	18%	9%	2%
Religious or faith-based community support	33%	36%	13%	7%	11%
Professional treatment	22%	45%	15%	7%	11%
Self-exclusion from casinos (register with casino)	24%	43%	22%	6%	6%
Recognition of shortcomings	22%	43%	17%	13%	6%
Gamblers Anonymous	28%	34%	24%	4%	11%

Source: Philip S. Kopel, Massachusetts Council on Compulsive Gambling, "Massachusetts Statewide Gambling Behavior, Opinions and Needs Assessment," 2013. http://50.87.144.117/~mccg/wp-content/uploads/2014/01/Massachusetts-Gambling-Behaviors-Opinions-and-Needs-Assessment-FINAL.pdf.

Key People and Advocacy Groups

Henrietta Bowden-Jones: A psychiatrist and neuroscience researcher, Bowden-Jones founded the NPGC, the first problem gambling clinic in the United Kingdom.

Casino Watch Focus: An online news blog dedicated to exposing problems associated with gambling.

Paul Davies: A journalist nominated for a Pulitzer Prize, Davies is the editor of *Get Government Out of Gambling*, a news blog against government-sponsored gambling.

Jeffrey L. Derevensky: A psychologist and professor at McGill University in Canada. Derevensky is the codirector of the International Centre for Youth Gambling Problems and High-Risk Behaviors and the recipient of the Joseph W. Ciarrocchi Problem Gambling Award, which recognizes pioneering research on youth problem gambling.

Gambling Reform and Society Perception: An independent reform group set up by former gambling addicts in the United Kingdom to raise awareness and restrict the damage done by gambling addiction.

Marilyn Lancelot: A recovering gambling addict, author of *Gripped by Gambling*, and founder of Women Helping Women, a support group for female gambling addicts. Lancelot started the first female-only meetings of GA.

National Coalition Against Legalized Gambling: A nonprofit educational group that educates the public about the detrimental effects of legalized gambling.

Howard Shaffer: A prominent academic researcher in the field of gambling addiction, Shaffer is the director of the Division on Addiction at Harvard Medical School.

Natasha Dow Schüll: A cultural anthropologist and professor at MIT, Schüll is the author of *Addiction by Design.*

Stop Predatory Gambling: A national reform group against government sponsorship of casinos and lotteries.

Arnie Wexler: The former executive director of the CCGNJ and a recovering gambling addict, Wexler trains and educates the gambling industry on how to spot gambling addiction.

Keith Whyte: The executive director of the NCPG and a noted speaker and author about problem gambling issues.

Chronology

1957
GA is founded in Los Angeles, California.

1980
Pathological gambling is listed in the *DSM-III*, which officially classifies it as a medical disease rather than a moral failing.

1989
The Mirage Hotel and Casino Resort opens in Las Vegas, the most expensive hotel casino in history. The Mirage was the first of many casino resorts that turned Las Vegas into a family vacation destination and legitimized gambling as entertainment.

1960 **1980**

1987
The South Oaks Gambling Screen questionnaire, the first scientific screening tool for pathological gambling, is developed.

1958
Gam-Anon, the support group for the friends and families of gambling addicts, is founded.

1988
The Indian Gaming Regulatory Act is passed, which leads to a rapid expansion of casinos operated by Native Americans.

1989
The Nevada Gaming Commission bans manipulation of slot machines to deliberately return a near miss (a result very close to a jackpot) because it encourages players to continue gambling.

1992
The first racino opens in Rhode Island. Racinos bring casino gambling to area racetracks, exposing more people to casino gaming machines.

1996
The AGA creates the NCRG to fund research on problem gambling.

2000
Casino manager and former gambling addict Bill Friedman publishes *Designing Casinos to Dominate the Competition.* Friedman's theories of how to encourage gambling by manipulating the environment influence the design of modern casinos.

2009
Kansas opens the first state-owned casino resort.

1990

2000

2010

1994
The *DSM-IV* defines pathological gambling as an impulse control disorder like kleptomania (compulsive theft) and pyromania (compulsive arson).

2003
The AGA enacts the AGA Code of Conduct for Responsible Gaming, which institutionalizes the AGA's claim that casinos do not intentionally exploit problem gamblers.

1999
The National Gambling Impact Study Commission, created by the US government in 1997, issues its final report. Most US statistics about gambling addiction are drawn from this report and from research funded by the NCRG.

2013
The term *pathological gambling* is renamed *gambling disorder* and is moved to a new behavioral addictions category in the *DSM-5.*

Related Organizations

American Gaming Association (AGA)
555 Thirteenth St. NW
Washington, DC 20004
phone: (202) 552-2679
e-mail: asmith@americangaming.org
website: www.americangaming.org

The AGA is the US gambling industry association. It lobbies on behalf of the industry in Washington, DC, and educates the public about gambling issues. Its website has information about gambling addiction and responsible gambling.

Casino-Free Philadelphia
PO Box 39766
Philadelphia, PA 19106
e-mail: info@casinofreephilly.org • website: www.casinofreephilly.org

Casino-Free Philadelphia is dedicated to fighting the predatory practices of casinos. Its website contains a wealth of facts and research about problem gambling.

Gamblers Anonymous (GA)
International Service Office
PO Box 17173
Los Angeles, CA 90017
phone: (213) 386-8789 • fax: (213) 386-0030
e-mail: isomain@gamblersanonymous.org
website: www.gamblersanonymous.org

GA is a nonprofit international 12-step program for problem gamblers and gambling addicts. Its website contains information and literature about gambling addiction.

Get Gambling Facts

1031 Portage Ave.

Winnipeg, MB R3G 0R8 Canada

phone: (800) 463-1554

website: getgamblingfacts.ca

Get Gambling Facts is part of the Addictions Foundation of Manitoba, a Canadian agency providing addiction services and education. The website has information, resources about problem gambling, and educational gambling simulators.

International Centre For Youth Gambling Problems and High-Risk Behaviors

McGill University

3724 McTavish Street

Montreal, QC H3A 1Y2 Canada

phone: (514) 398-1391 • fax: (514) 398-3401

e-mail: ygi.educ@mcgill.ca • website: www.youthgambling.com

This organization is involved in research, prevention, and the training of professionals concerned with youth gambling and treatment. Its website has information for adolescents and parents about problem gambling, as well as links to research studies and articles on problem gambling and youth.

KnowTheOdds.org

100 Great Oaks Blvd., Suite 126

Albany, NY 12203

phone: (518) 867-4084

e-mail: council@nyproblemgambling.org

website: http://knowtheodds.org

KnowTheOdds.org is part of the NYCPG's public awareness campaign on problem gambling. The website has resources, videos, e-books, and a blog with information about gambling addiction.

Massachusetts Council on Compulsive Gambling
190 High St., Suite 5
Boston, MA 02110
phone: (617) 426-4554 • fax: (617) 426-4555
e-mail: info@masscompulsivegambling.org
website: www.masscompulsivegambling.org

The Massachusetts Council on Compulsive Gambling is a private, non-profit health agency that provides education and training about problem gambling. Its website contains podcasts, fact sheets, a blog, and useful links about gambling addiction.

National Center for Responsible Gaming (NCRG)
900 Cummings Ctr., Suite 216-U
Beverly, MA 01915
phone: (978) 338-6610 • fax: (978) 552-8452
e-mail: info@ncrg.org • website: www.ncrg.org

The NCRG was formed by the AGA in 1996 to fund research into gambling and gambling disorders. Its website contains a research library, webinars, videos, and a link to *The Wager,* a monthly online review of worldwide research into gambling addiction.

National Council on Problem Gambling (NCPG)
730 Eleventh St. NW, Suite 601
Washington, DC 20001
phone: (202) 547-9204
e-mail: ncpg@ncpgambling.org • website: www.ncpgambling.org

The NCPG is the national advocate for education, programs, and services to assist problem gamblers. Its website contains educational resources about problem gambling.

Nevada Council on Problem Gambling
5552 S. Fort Apache Rd., Suite 100
Las Vegas, NV 89148
phone: (702) 369-9740
e-mail: info@nevadacouncil.org • website: www.nevadacouncil.org

The Nevada Council on Problem Gambling generates awareness, promotes education, and advocates for quality treatment of problem gambling. Its website has information and links about problem gambling and responsible gaming.

UCLA Gambling Studies Program (UGSP)

760 Westwood Plaza, 3rd Floor, Suite 38-181
Los Angeles, CA 90024
phone: (310) 825-4845
e-mail: ugsp@mednet.ucla.edu • website: www.uclagamblingprogram.org

The UGSP conducts research and provides education about problem gambling. Its website contains information, links, and bibliographies about problem gambling.

For Further Research

Books
Jeffrey Derevensky, *Teen Gambling: Understanding a Growing Epidemic.* New York: Rowman & Littlefield, 2012.

Sally Gainsbury, *Internet Gambling: Current Research Findings and Implications.* New York: Springer Science, 2012.

Justyn Rees Larcombe, *Tails I Lose: The Compulsive Gambler Who Lost His Shirt for Good.* Oxford, UK: Lion Hudson, 2014.

Jake Ploeth, *Gambling Addiction.* Johnstown, CO: JK, 2012.

Natasha Dow Schüll, *Addiction by Design: Machine Gambling in Las Vegas.* Princeton, NJ: Princeton University Press, 2012.

Sam Skolnik, *High Stakes: The Rising Cost of America's Gambling Addiction.* Boston: Beacon, 2011.

Lisa Ustok and Joanna Hughes, *First Steps Out of Problem Gambling.* Oxford, UK: Lion Hudson, 2011.

Periodicals
Les Bernal, "Why Don't Casino Advocates and Executives Patronize Casinos?," *New Hampshire Union Leader,* March 11, 2014.

Daniel Bortz, "Gambling Addiction Affects More Men and Women, Seduced by Growing Casino Accessibility," *New York Daily News,* March 28, 2013.

Economist, "Gambling and the Brain: Slotting in an Explanation," March 15, 2014.

Steve Fox, "This Is Why You Should Talk to Your Kids About Gambling Addiction," *Denver Post,* March 26, 2014.

Martin Fridson, "Don't Bet on Internet Gambling Ban," *Forbes,* April 22, 2014.

Ferris Jabr, "How the Brain Gets Addicted to Gambling," *Scientific American,* October 15, 2013.

Simon Murphy, "Escape from Gambling Hell," *Guardian* (Manchester, UK), April 20, 2012.

Alice Robb, "Why Are Slot Machines So Addictive?," *New Republic*, December 5, 2013.

Natasha Dow Schüll, "Slot Machines Are Designed to Addict," *New York Times*, October 10, 2013.

Barbara DaFoe Whitehead, "Gaming the Poor," *New York Times,* June 21, 2014.

Internet Sources

Sanju George and Henrietta Bowden-Jones, *Gambling: The Hidden Addiction*, Royal College of Psychiatrists, April 2014. www.rcpsych .ac.uk/pdf/FR%20AP%2001-for%20websiteApril2014.pdf.

Keren Henderson, "Gambling Preys on the Poor," Cincinnati.com, March 22, 2014. www.cincinnati.com/story/opinion/columnists /2014/03/22/opinion-gambling-preys-poor/6733285.

Raanan Kagan et al., *Problem Gambling in the 21st Century Healthcare System*, National Council on Problem Gambling, July 3, 2014. www .ncpgambling.org/wp-content/uploads/2014/07/ACA-brief-web -layout-publication.pdf.

Jana Kasperkevic, "You Can Tell by Age 3 Who Will Be a Gambler When They Grow Up," Business Insider, April 10, 2012. www.businessin sider.com/wendy-slutskes-paper-on-potential-gamblers-2012-4.

KnowTheOdds.org, *The Dangers of Youth Gambling Addiction,* May 2013. PDF e-book. http://knowtheodds.org/wp-content/uploads/2013/05 /NYCPG_ebook_YouthGambling_052114.pdf.

I. Nelson Rose, "Compulsive Gambler Just Can't Win," Gambling and the Law, 2011. www.gamblingandthelaw.com/index.php/columns /288-compulsive-gambler-just-cant-win21.

Alice K. Ross, "Gambling: The Secret Addiction," Bureau of Investigative Journalism, July 24, 2012. www.thebureauinvestigates .com/2012/07/24/gambling-the-secret-addiction.

TEDMED Live Royal Albert Hall, "Treating Addiction Against All Odds: Henrietta Bowden-Jones at TEDMEDLive Imperial College 2013," YouTube video, May 21, 2013. www.youtube.com /watch?v=58zvtB4GHZY.

US Department of Health and Human Services, "Maturation of the Prefrontal Cortex," Bridges 2 Understanding, March 5, 2013. http:// bridges2understanding.com/maturation-of-the-prefrontal-cortex.

Keith Whyte, letter to the Senate Subcommittee on Consumer Protection, Product Safety & Insurance, National Council on Problem Gambling, July 12, 2013. www.ncpgambling.org/wp-content/up loads/2014/08/Senate-Commerce-Committee-letter-re-internet -gambing-and-consumer-protection.pdf.

Source Notes

Overview

1. Quoted in Ferris Jabr, "How the Brain Gets Addicted to Gambling," *Scientific American,* October 15, 2013. www.scientificamerican.com.
2. Quoted in Jabr, "How the Brain Gets Addicted to Gambling."
3. Massachusetts Council on Compulsive Gambling, "Gambling Disorders and Substance Abuse Disorders," March 5, 2014. www.masscompulsivegambling.org.
4. Quoted in Natasha Dow Schüll, *Addiction by Design: Machine Gambling in Las Vegas.* Princeton, NJ: Princeton University Press, 2012. Kindle edition.
5. Quoted in Schüll, *Addiction by Design.*
6. Quoted in Steve Fox, "This Is Why You Should Talk to Your Kids About Gambling Addiction," *Denver Post,* March 26, 2014. www.denverpost.com.
7. Keith Whyte, letter to the Senate Subcommittee on Consumer Protection, Product Safety & Insurance, National Council on Problem Gambling, July 12, 2013. www.ncpgambling.org.
8. Quoted in Schüll, *Addiction by Design.*
9. Schüll, *Addiction by Design.*
10. Raanan Kagan et al., *Problem Gambling in the 21st Century Healthcare System,* National Council on Problem Gambling, July 3, 2014. www.ncpgambling.org.

What Is Gambling Addiction?

11. Quoted in TEDMED Live Royal Albert Hall, "Treating Addiction Against All Odds: Henrietta Bowden-Jones at TEDMEDLive Imperial College 2013," YouTube video, May 21, 2013. www.youtube.com.
12. Quoted in Schüll, *Addiction by Design.*
13. Quoted in Jana Kasperkevic, "You Can Tell by Age 3 Who Will Be a Gambler When They Grow Up," Business Insider, April 10, 2012. www.businessinsider.com.
14. Quoted in Cathy Wilde, "People in Poor Neighborhoods Are Twice as Likely to Have Gambling Problems, Study Finds," University at Buffalo News Center, January 3, 2014. www.buffalo.edu.
15. American Gaming Association, "Does Casino Gambling Prey on the Poor and the Elderly?," 2014. www.americangaming.org.
16. Quoted in Heather Larson, "Avoiding the Pitfalls of Gambling After 50," *Forbes,* July 17, 2014. www.forbes.com.
17. KnowTheOdds.org, *The Dangers of Youth Gambling Addiction,* May 2013. PDF e-book. http://knowtheodds.org.
18. US Department of Health and Human Services, "Maturation of the Prefrontal Cortex," Bridges 2 Understanding, March 5, 2013. http://bridges2understanding.com.
19. Quoted in Jeffrey L. Derevensky, *Teen Gambling: Understanding a Growing Epidemic.* Plymouth, UK: Rowman & Littlefield, 2012, p. 54.

Why Do People Become Addicted to Gambling?

20. American Gaming Association, "Casino Expansion and Its Impact on Pathological and Problem Gambling Prevalence Rates," 2014. www.americangaming.org.

21. Schüll, *Addiction by Design.*
22. Quoted in Jabr, "How the Brain Gets Addicted to Gambling."
23. Quoted in Alice Robb, "Why Are Slot Machines So Addictive?," *New Republic*, December 5, 2013. www.newrepublic.com.
24. Quoted in Schüll, *Addiction by Design.*
25. Quoted in Schüll, *Addiction by Design.*
26. Quoted in Schüll, *Addiction by Design.*
27. Keren Henderson, "Gambling Preys on the Poor," Cincinnati.com, March 22, 2014. www.cincinnati.com.
28. Quoted in Schüll, *Addiction by Design.*
29. Natasha Dow Schüll, "Slot Machines Are Designed to Addict," *New York Times,* October 10, 2013. www.nytimes.com.
30. Quoted in Schüll, "Slot Machines Are Designed to Addict."
31. Quoted in Schüll, *Addiction by Design.*

What Are the Costs of Gambling Addiction?

32. Quoted in "Tunbridge Wells Man Lost £750,000 Gambling Online," BBC News Kent, August 2, 2013. www.bbc.com.
33. Quoted in John Domokos et al., "FOBTs: 'The Crack Cocaine of Gambling,'" *Guardian* video, April 6, 2014. www.theguardian.com.
34. Quoted in Simon Murphy, "Escape from Gambling Hell," *Guardian,* April 20, 2012. www.theguardian.com.
35. Quoted in TEDMED Live Royal Albert Hall, "Treating Addiction Against All Odds."
36. Philip Mawer, "Paying the Ultimate Price for My Gambling," *Gamblersaloud* (blog). www.gamblersaloud.com.
37. Quoted in TEDMED Live Royal Albert Hall, "Treating Addiction Against All Odds."
38. Paul Davies, "A Dirty Secret: Suicides at Casinos," *Get Government Out of Gambling* (blog), February 8, 2014. www.getgovernmentoutofgambling.org.
39. Paul Davies, "The Casino Crime Blotter," *Get Government Out of Gambling* (blog), December 31, 2013. www.getgovernmentoutofgambling.org.
40. Quoted in Larson, "Avoiding the Pitfalls of Gambling After 50."
41. Quoted in Alice K. Ross, "Gambling: The Secret Addiction," Bureau of Investigative Journalism, July 24, 2012. www.thebureauinvestigates.com.

Can Gambling Addiction Be Overcome?

42. Brad Girtz, "Residential Treatment for Gambling Addiction: 5 Things to Look For," AddictionBlog.org, September 27, 2013. http://gambling.addictionblog.org.
43. Quoted in TEDMED Live Royal Albert Hall, "Treating Addiction Against All Odds."
44. Quoted in Eliot Barford, "Dedicated to Mending Broken Lives," Imperial College London News, August 19, 2013. www3.imperial.ac.uk.
45. Sanju George and Henrietta Bowden-Jones, *Gambling: The Hidden Addiction*, Royal College of Psychiatrists, April 2014. www.rcpsych.ac.uk.
46. Quoted in Kathryn Hecht, "Gambling Addiction: Out of Blame and into Funding," Freedom Institute, September 24, 2012. www.freedominstitute.org.
47. Substance Abuse and Mental Health Services Administration, "SAMHSA Announces a Working Definition of 'Recovery' from Mental Disorders and Substance Use Disorders," December 22, 2011. www.samhsa.gov.

48. Quoted in Sam Skolnik, *High Stakes: The Rising Cost of America's Gambling Addiction.* Boston: Beacon, 2011. Kindle edition.

49. Quoted in Sarah Ottney, "Casino Plans Events for Responsible Gaming Week," *Toledo Free Press,* August 2, 2014. www.toledofreepress.com.

50. American Gaming Association, "Are Pathological Gamblers the Main Source of Revenue for Casinos?," 2014. www.americangaming.org.

51. Quoted in Associated Press, "Experts Help Casinos Spot Compulsive Gamblers," *USA Today,* February 26, 2012. http://usatoday30.usatoday.com.

52. Quoted in Associated Press, "Experts Help Casinos Spot Compulsive Gamblers."

53. Quoted in TEDMED Live Royal Albert Hall, "Treating Addiction Against All Odds."

List of Illustrations

Index

Note: Boldface page numbers indicate illustrations.

About the Author

Christine Wilcox writes fiction and nonfiction for young adults and adults. She has worked as an editor, an instructional designer, and a writing instructor. She lives in Richmond, Virginia, with her husband, David, and her son, Doug.